What people are saying about

The End of Capitalism: The Thought of Henryk Grossman

Revealing the richness of the Marxist tradition, Reese provides an illuminating introduction into the life an   ight of Henryk Grossman, connecting his many in   'e dynamics of capitalism, its contradictions   'o produce economic crises to present-d
Asatar Bair, Associate   .verside City College, author of *Pris*   *conomic Analysis*

The End of Capitalism coul.   more urgent for socialists. In outlining the looming ine..ability of capitalist breakdown, Reese makes a compelling case for Grossman's work to be considered required reading alongside Marxist giants like Engels, Lenin and Trotsky.
Stephen Radecki, The Swoletariat

The rescuing of Henryk Grossman from obscurity is indispensable for any attempt to understand and overcome the crises confronting us today. Reese has written an inspiring and electrifying book.
James Bell, Prolekult

Reese offers a fresh perspective on an underrated figure in the Marxist canon and shows how much fresher our perspectives could be if we gave Grossman the attention he has wrongly been denied.
Kali Koba, Desperate Times Blog

Reese navigates what could easily be a series of complicated economic theories with his typical aptitude, making them accessible to amateur economists and laymen alike. He clearly demonstrates the significant value of Grossman's contribution to Marxist economics. Indeed, Grossman's writings now seem stunningly prescient.

wielisc, The Next Left

The End of Capitalism: The Thought of Henryk Grossman

Also by the author
Socialism or Extinction: Climate, Automation and War in the
Final Capitalist Breakdown
ISBN: 9798554968730

The End of Capitalism: The Thought of Henryk Grossman

Ted Reese

Winchester, UK
Washington, USA

JOHN HUNT PUBLISHING

First published by Zero Books, 2022
Zero Books is an imprint of John Hunt Publishing Ltd., No. 3 East St., Alresford,
Hampshire SO24 9EE, UK
office@jhpbooks.com
www.johnhuntpublishing.com
www.zero-books.net

For distributor details and how to order please visit the 'Ordering' section on our website.

ISBN: 978 1 78904 773 8
978 1 78904 774 5 (ebook)
Library of Congress Control Number: 2021932925

A CIP catalogue record for this book is available from the British Library.

Design: Stuart Davies

UK: Printed and bound by CPI Group (UK) Ltd, Croydon, CR0 4YY
Printed in North America by CPI GPS partners

We operate a distinctive and ethical publishing philosophy in
all areas of our business, from our global network of authors to
production and worldwide distribution.

Contents

Acknowledgements

For their proofreading, constructive criticism, encouragement and support, my heartfelt thanks go to Maria Mudzanga, James Bell and especially Luke Beesley, whose comprehensive knowledge and occasional translations of Grossman's work have been invaluable.

My thanks also to the team at Zer0 Books/John Hunt Publishing, especially Ashley Frawley for taking interest in my first, little-known, self-published book, and suggesting this one; John Romans for his copy-editing; and Andrew Wells, Dominic James and Douglas Lain for patiently answering all my questions.

Introduction

Henryk Grossman is a name most socialists or students of political and social theory, let alone the mass of working people around the world, have probably never heard of. Yet Grossman, a Polish Jew born in 1881, deserves recognition as the most sophisticated proponent since Karl Marx of a devastating claim about the nature of our social world. For, if Grossman's neglected but brilliant insight into economics is correct, then capitalism – the social system that has dominated life all over the globe for the past few centuries – may well be entering what he called its 'final breakdown'.

The claim that capitalism is unsustainable has been ridiculed since the collapse of the Soviet Union in 1991. Capitalists declared 'the end of history' – their system had proven to be the stronger and would go on uncontested until the heat death of the universe. The same view dominated after the 1883 death of Marx, whose three-volume masterpiece *Capital* exposed capitalism as a crisis-ridden and historically transient economic system (mode of production).

For the next half century even Marx's self-proclaimed successors either declared capitalism to be crisis-free and inexhaustible, or formulated flawed theories of crisis and collapse that did not support their own claims. Against the grain, Grossman dedicated himself to restoring the basis of scientific socialism. In 1929 he illuminated Marx's insights with a rare clarity and wit in his own great work, *The Law of Accumulation and Breakdown of the Capitalist System*, published in 1929.

The book received an almost universally hostile reception. Attacked by both reformist social democrats and revolutionary communists, Grossman stood accused of promoting a 'mechanical' or 'automatic' theory of socialism's 'inevitable' victory over capitalism that underplayed the importance of class struggle. Neither allegation is substantiated. Grossman not only gave the most thorough account of capitalism's ability to rejuvenate but re-established the indissoluble link between economic dynamics and class struggle. In doing so he complemented and supplemented the revolutionary politics of Marxism already recovered by Vladimir Lenin, the leader of the 1917 Russian Revolution. Far from a soulless prophecy of capitalism's automatic collapse into socialism, Grossman sought to interrogate the conditions under which we (as people, classes, social groups) make our own history, with a specific emphasis on the conditions which are not of any of our choosing.

To say that the communist movement of his time under-appreciated Grossman is to put things mildly, yet his work remains largely neglected in contemporary discussions of Marxist theory. Recent efforts to assert the importance of Grossman's thought cuts against academic reluctance to engage with capitalism as a structure of the world rather than of thought; and against the belief of many left-wing activists that capitalism should be mended, not ended. Most notably, Australian Marxist Rick Kuhn's remarkable biography of Grossman and ongoing translation of his collected works from Polish, Yiddish and German foreground Grossman as the most insightful Marxist economist of the twentieth century.

Before Kuhn's work, only an abridged version of *The Law of Accumulation* had been translated into English, and not until 1992.[1] This book seeks to contribute to the project of recovering Grossman's insights for a new generation of socialists and revolutionaries by introducing the central tenets of Grossman's thought and applying them to the present – quite possibly, final – capitalist crisis.

While the following chapters put forth Grossman's most important interventions in the realm of both economics and politics, a brief discussion here of his breakdown theory, in relation to the current crisis, will help orientate the reader towards his central concerns.

Most critically, Grossman upheld Marx's contention that capitalism – a social system based on the private ownership of production and capital accumulation; i.e., the reinvestment of profit in new production – a) derives its growth from the exploitation of human labour; b) suffers regular economic contractions due to inherent contradictions, resulting in surplus capital that cannot be (re)invested profitably; c) *necessarily* depresses working-class living standards in order to counter this problem; and d) cannot go on forever.

Historically, capitalism has overcome downturns by restructuring itself in order to return to growth on a higher level: failing businesses (or even whole industries) disappear; their assets are sold at bargain prices to surviving firms that monopolise, expand and cheapen production; and workers are compelled to accept lower wages and worse conditions.

Up to now, such tendencies – alongside colonial expansion – have limited crises, to one degree or another, to partial and temporary economic breakdowns. Grossman, however, warns of an eventual final breakdown that will *compel* the working masses to take up a revolutionary struggle for political power and a higher, sustainable mode of production – socialism.

* * *

Fast forward a century and capitalism finally seems to be reaching this point. In March 2020, stock markets crashed harder in relative terms than at any point during the Great Depression that started in 1929. Many countries in Sub-Saharan Africa and Latin America were already in recession (two back-to-back 3-month periods of contraction), while Germany and Britain were spluttering along at near-zero growth.

Far from causing the crash, news of the Covid-19 pandemic (and the unprecedented worldwide social 'lockdowns' that followed) served merely as a catalyst. Stock markets (where individual and institutional investors buy and sell shares in companies) would not have tumbled by 30% if the value of stocks had not been epically over-valued (selling for much more than their real worth), forming a financial 'bubble' that was sooner or later bound to burst. Stock prices in the US, the world's long-time economic superpower, had been at a record high of 150% of Gross Domestic Product (GDP) – the average is 50% – and were extremely vulnerable to an external shock.

After the start of social lockdowns that governments mandated in the name of suppressing the virus, hundreds of millions of people around the world lost their livelihoods or much of their income.[2] The United Nations (UN) warned of famines 'of biblical proportions'. Crude oil prices *fell below zero for the first time ever.*

The situation has been met with an unprecedented cocktail of government spending (bail-outs, loan programmes, other subsidies for capital, and enforcing lockdowns) and zero interest rates – along with the accelerated privatisation of health care and education – much of it funded by record levels of central bank money printing. Global debt keeps hitting new highs.

Britain, the oldest capitalist superpower, entered its worst recession since 1709, its economy shrinking by 25% in March and April 2020. The World Bank estimated in June 2020 that global production would contract by 5.2% for the year, from $89.94 trillion to $83.19 trillion – equivalent to the output of Germany and France combined – three times worse than the 1.7% during the so-called Great Recession (2007-09) that nearly all 'mainstream' economists failed to anticipate (or, rather, warn of). Investment in the poorer 'developing' countries by capitalists based in the richer 'developed' countries initially fell five-fold compared to that previous crisis.[3] In November, Zambia became the sixth country to default or restructure debts in 2020. The International Monetary Fund estimated that global

GDP in 2025 would be 31% worse off than had been projected before 2007.

After lockdowns began to ease (before being re-tightened), economies began to grow again, albeit from a significantly smaller base (the UK economy remained 7% smaller at the end of 2020 compared to a year earlier). The stock markets, based on the growth of a small number of multi- and transnational tech conglomerates, soared back to record highs. The financial bubble that had been forming over the past decade reinflated to an even larger size and the World Bank predicted growth would return to 4.1% in 2021 (revised down in April 2021 to 3.3%). So what evidence is there to suggest that capitalism may have entered the process of a breakdown it cannot recover from?

For starters, this financial bubble is unlike any that has gone before. Finance analyst Graham Summers has called it 'the everything bubble' (the title of his 2017 book) and the third 'one-in-100 year' bubble in three successive decades. The 1990s and 2000s were 'only' beset by 'the internet/tech bubble' and 'the housing bubble', respectively. Now:

> the bedrock of the entire global financial system (US Treasuries) [has] entered a bubble forcing all other asset classes to adjust accordingly...[4]
>
> The bubble comprises numerous smaller, individual debt bubbles...bubbles in corporate debt, municipal debt, consumer debt, commercial debt, etc. As such, the entire $60 trillion in debt securities floating around the US financial system is vulnerable to debt deflation when the bubble bursts...[5]

Whereas the size of the US tech bubble reached $7 trillion and the US housing bubble twice that, the US bond bubble has surpassed $20 trillion. 'When you include junior [lower priority] debt instruments and derivatives [bets on future prices] associated with bond yields, the figure rises to $124 trillion.'[6] To put that in perspective, total global wealth in 2019 stood at $360 trillion.

That capitalism is entering its deepest ever crisis is indicated perhaps even more starkly by the fact that base interest rates (the rate of borrowing targeted by central banks) have long been stuck at or near zero – when ending a recession usually requires an average 6% cut.[7]

Interest rates have been trending downwards towards zero since the fifteenth century.[8] Having never gone below 0.64% before 2010,[9] the Fed held its target rate at zero for 7 years following the Great Recession. After going back up to 2.25% between 2016 and 2019, the rate was cut to 1.75% in 2019 and then 0% after the March 2020 crash. In Britain the rate had never gone below 2% before 2010, but has been more or less held at zero ever since.

To be clear, with rates at zero borrowers only have to pay back what they were lent. Interest rate cuts lower borrowing repayments, stimulating the cash flow needed to keep business and the economy in general running; and making the repayment of government debt more affordable. Even at 0%, however, central banks have been inundated by retailers and borrowers to lower rates to offset deflation, a general fall of prices that affects the ability and confidence of investors, homeowners and banks to spend and lend.[10]

Private banks have warned that negative rates threaten their profitability,[11] yet the alternative may be the total implosion of the global financial bubble – along with the international banking system. To keep short-term rates going down, more and more debt has to be issued. To bring longer-term rates down (i.e., to raise demand for long-term debt), more and more cash needs to be converted into stocks, raising prices and lowering yields (rates). The bubble is now so big that this would likely involve increasingly unprecedented levels of money printing; bans on high denomination bills and charges on carrying smaller denominations; taxes on net wealth; and 'bail-ins',[12] whereby banks – instead of being bailed-out by an outside source – seize customer assets or convert them into stocks.

Negative rates also mean that banks charge customers to deposit cash with them in the first place, while borrowers of government debt receive less back than the amount they lent. This has already started to happen in Europe and Japan over the past decade, but has never before happened in the US and Britain, capitalism's historical leading powers.

Negative rates are of course incredibly politically toxic and must eventually disincentive bond-holding. Investors (individual or institutional) are confronted, however, with the choice of losing some of their investment or all of it.

When the bubble finally implodes, most major banks will go bankrupt; governments across the world – and large corporations – will default on their debt (fail to repay it); many, many companies and investors will go bust; pensions will evaporate; spending on public services will hit rock bottom; and unemployment will explode to all-time record highs, probably in relative as well as absolute terms.

Negative rates, even if they are tolerated for a time, cannot go down forever. When governments and central banks run out of ways to convert cash into stocks, interest rates will start to rise again, at some point triggering panic selling on the stock markets as investors realise that governments cannot afford to repay their debts. Central banks will have to print yet more money to buy dumped bonds. Put simply, it's a recipe – since the US dollar is the global reserve currency[13] – for worldwide hyperinflation.

Abnormally high inflation (above 2%) occurs if: the total of all goods and services demanded exceeds production; the amount of all goods and services supplied by producers decreases; or the supply of currency becomes significantly higher than demand for that currency. Since demand for currency rises in a crisis, a match in supply via printing is required and deflation is prevented or limited. If, however, demand falls or collapses due to bankruptcies and high or mass unemployment, and the supply goes up in an effort to raise prices or boost consumption, then inflation becomes abnormally high. This is now the risk, since bonds held by central banks would normally be sold back to the private market before inflation becomes a problem – but the private sector is also increasingly dependent on central banks as the purchaser of corporate bonds.

Even though central banks have become by far the largest buyers of government (public) debt, cancelling a government's debt to its central bank is not much of an option. Firstly, as Bank of England (BoE) governor Andrew Bailey – who has had to reject accusations about pursuing monetary financing, a term associated with hyperinflation – pointed out, government borrowing from the central bank cannot be cost-free, since the BoE is still paying interest on reserves.[14] Secondly, the factoring-in of future debt repayments in spending plans helps prevent the sort of high inflation that would otherwise result from such a rapid expansion in the money supply.

In August, the chief US equity strategist at US multinational investment firm Morgan Stanley, Mike Wilson, admitted that the Federal Reserve, 'may not be in control of money supply growth, which means [it] won't have control of inflation either, if it gets going'.[15]

Everything points to the US dollar collapsing against precious metals. When high inflation will turn into hyperinflation exactly is impossible to tell, but we may well be talking within the decade. Hyperinflation can be avoided only if the Fed accepts the inevitability of the bubble bursting and gives up on monetary financing, thereby triggering hyperdeflation, which would follow hyperinflation anyway.

The prospect of worldwide hyperinflation fits logically with the historical devaluation of fiat (unbacked paper) currency.

The US dollar lost more than 97% of its purchasing power between 1635 and 2019, but this devaluation has tended to accelerate – the figure is 96% when the starting point is taken from 1913, having remained nearly unchanged in the previous 120 years;[16] 91% from 1947, when the US became the world's leading capitalist power; and 85% since 1970, around the time the postwar productivity boom ended.[17] For British pound sterling, the figure is more than 99.5% compared to 1694, the year it was adopted as the Royal Chartered Bank of England's currency.[18]

As John Smith, author of *Imperialism in the Twenty-First Century*, has written:

> In the end, dollar bills, like bond and share certificates, are just pieces of paper. As trillions more of them flood into the system, events in March 2020 bring closer the day when investors will lose faith in cash itself – and in the power of the economy and state standing behind it...capitalism cannot escape from this crisis, no matter how many trillions of dollars governments borrow or central banks print. The trillions they spent after 2007-9 bought another decade of zombie-like life for their vile system...The coronavirus [crisis] makes socialist revolution...across the world into a necessity.[19]

* * *

That zero rates are converging with exhausted major currencies at the end of a decade in which the deindustrialisation of the global workforce has been more or less completed – shifting employment predominantly from manufacturing to services – can be no coincidence, for capital's exploitation of commodity-producing human labour is the sole source of the production of exchange-value and profit. While the mass of profit produced tends to continue to rise absolutely during capitalist development, as production becomes more mechanised and automated, the value-producing component in the production process (human labour) tends to diminish. The *rate* at which profit is produced relative to the total value of capital therefore *tends* to fall.

The general rate of profit trends downwards not just in cycles of years or decades, but historically towards zero. A study in 2014 confirmed this fact, estimating that the general rate of profit in the 'advanced' economies is on course to reach zero in 2054, having fallen in an overall trend from an approximate decade average of 43% in the 1870s to 17% in the 2000s.[20] As Grossman warns, however: 'There is an absolute limit to the accumulation of capital and this limit comes into force much earlier than a zero rate of profit.'[21]

This is because the total mass of capital, as it grows larger and larger, becomes increasingly difficult to 'valorise' – that is, reproduce (preserve in value) *and* expand. At the same time, the pool of exploitable labour dwindles in relation to total capital. If labour comprises 30% of the productive forces and machinery 70%, then the former's ability to valorise capital is much greater than if it only comprises 10%. The remaining 10% would have to work much harder.

Until now, this contradiction has resulted in a periodic (on average once per decade) *partial* 'overaccumulation' of capital, which is at the same time an underproduction of profit. This surplus capital cannot be (re)invested because it cannot yield a higher return, thereby placing a fetter (restraint) on investment and productivity growth. Counter-actions must be taken by the capitalist class to sufficiently devalue and centralise capital, restoring accumulation on a higher level. This is achieved during the crisis through wage reductions, innovation, company mergers, and so on. A final breakdown, though, implies an *absolute* overaccumulation of capital – whereby the counter-tendencies come up against definite limits, *all* accumulation ceases, attacks on wages and conditions go into overdrive and production begins to grind to a halt.

Eventually accumulation itself demands a new, higher mode of production that removes the fetters on productivity – privately-owned production, surplus capital and the profit motive. This higher mode of production is socialism, a system that replaces privately-owned, for-profit commodity production with socially-owned, break-even utility production (production based on needs and wants); and money with vouchers pegged to labour time. In the long run, this system will bring about abundant material wealth *for all*, leading to the withering away of all classes and states, i.e., communism.

* * *

Grossman's elaboration of Marx has been consistently ignored, his central claims mischaracterised and his revolutionary theory derided. His work proved to be too radical for both the reformists of social democracy and the Soviet leadership (for whom it undermined their foreign policy of peaceful co-existence).

It seems, however, that Grossman's warning is now more relevant than ever. That Marx's true economics could have been lost for good without his contribution makes Grossman as important to today's burgeoning revolutionary movement as Lenin, Mao, Luxemburg, Lukacs and other revolutionaries whose work is being re-evaluated in light of contemporary events. He must be rehabilitated.

Chapter 1

The Life and Politics of Henryk Grossman, Part 1

Despite his privileged upbringing and education, Henryk Grossman began to identify as a socialist from the age of 15. On May Day 1896, only the sixth annual International Workers' Day, Grossman followed Gallacian working men into a local meeting hall outraged by the presence of occupying Habsburg soldiers in the autonomous Polish region. Once inside, he crawled through the legs of attendees to hear speakers at the front arguing for socialism. Inspired, Grossman 'rapidly mastered all the Marxist literature' according to his own, typically modest, account.[22]

At around the same time, his father, a small mine owner, passed away unexpectedly. The family remained financially comfortable and continued to live in Krakow, where Henryk, originally named Chaskel, had been born. While registered as Jewish, the change of the young Grossman's name epitomised his parents' assimilation into polite Polish society.[23] Krakow was the cultural capital of Poland – then partitioned between Russia, the Habsburg Empire and Germany – and the administrative centre and commercial hub of western Galicia, a province of the Austro-Hungarian Empire.

Grossman's Jewishness played a critical role in his political development. Thanks to its wealth, his family was relatively insulated from the anti-semitic bigotry and discrimination that blighted working-class Jewish life. Like his parents, Grossman enjoyed the cultural pursuits of the fashionable upper classes, but despite this and his schooling at an elite Polish boarding school, Grossman could not ignore a rising political antisemitism that bred some sense of cross-class resistance among Jewish people.

He would later write that this growing antisemitism was driven to some extent by capitalist penetration into the countryside and the ensuing attacks on traditional Jewish roles.[24]

Under Austrian law, Jews were defined as a religious group with equal civil rights to any other. The vast majority of Jews in Galicia, however, who were poor and spoke Yiddish as their first language, were disadvantaged even compared to poor Poles.[25] Yiddish was not recognised as a language and Jews were hardly represented in public service, the judiciary or universities. This dispossessed group, speaking a different language and increasingly present in poor urban neighbourhoods, became a convenient scapegoat for the ruling class, who wanted to displace the anger of Polish workers at exploitative labour practices and foreign rule.

Having previously described himself as Jewish by religion and Polish by nationality, in his second semester of university Grossman put a dash under 'Nationality' on his enrolment form. After studying law and philosophy, he disappointed his mother by turning down her wish for him to take on responsibilities in the family business.[26]

Grossman had become active as a young radical in the production of a political student magazine in 1899. By the end of the decade, he had taken on the socialist leaders of Galicia in a theoretical debate at a conference[27] – and by the age of 24 he had founded a new party.

Anti-war activism

The Polish Social Democratic Party (PPSD), like its peers in the Second International[28] (the international organisation of socialist parties), had committed itself to reforming Polish society through the ballot. They hoped to bring together Polish speaking regions in different empires through loose electoral alliances across borders. Although the International was formally Marxist, the wing which dominated most European parties rejected Marx's revolutionary road to socialism: in place of the abolition of the bourgeois (capitalist) state and its replacement by a socialist state, they advocated a path to socialism through legal reforms and the liberties already afforded workers, such as the rights to vote, unionise and assemble. Grossman was a member of the PPSD but vocally challenged the leadership.

He also joined and became vice-president (and then secretary) of Ruch (Movement), the main organisation of radical and socialist students in Krakow.[29] It was associated not only with the PPSD but also the Polish Socialist Party (PPS), led by Józef Pilsudski; and the Social Democracy of the Kingdom of Poland and Lithuania (SDKPiL), led by the revolutionary Rosa Luxemburg. Grossman identified with the SDKPiL,[30] which supported not only Jewish and Ukrainian minority rights but also the rights of persecuted Poles in Prussia's Polish territories, where they were made to conduct all education in German. Ruch was never large, peaking at 110 members in 1903, but it was involved in building trade unions, with Grossman focusing on organising Yiddish-speaking workers.

Among the lectures and debates organised by Ruch, one was addressed by Bronislaw Grosser, a member of the General Jewish Workers Union of Lithuania, Poland and Russia (better known as the Bund), then the largest Marxist organisation in the Russian Empire. He brought news of the revival of mass social unrest in Russia, which was losing the Russo-Japanese War that had begun in February 1904.[31]

Grossman was at the forefront of Ruch's efforts to smuggle the SDKPiL's anti-war literature into the Kingdom of Poland (later doing the same for Bundist pamphlets.) In February 1904, he also joined the Krakow branch of the Fund for the Assistance of Political Prisoners and Exiles, an organisation of SDKPiL members and sympathisers supporting socialists victimised by the counter-revolution in Russia. Kuhn reports that, 'His house acted as a hub for the flow of information into and out of Russia and was on the route of political refugees fleeing the autocracy.'[32]

Challenging chauvinism: The Grossman affair

The Bund and the SDKPiL, along with the left wings of the PPS and PPSD, called for working- class unity across national lines and saw it as their duty to support the intention of the Russian social democrats to bring down the Tsar. But independence remained the absolute priority for the PPS and PPSD leaderships. Frustrated activists in Ruch broke from the PPS-dominated *Promien*, the main organ of socialist students in Poland, to launch *Zjednoczenie* (*Unification*). Grossman became the responsible editor and publisher.[33]

The editorial of the first issue of the journal in February 1905 proclaimed that, unlike the PPS and PPSD, 'we won't just tolerate Ruthenians [Ukrainians] or deny Jews the right to self-determination. People who regard themselves as a nation are a nation. This is the only rational argument.'[34]

In a series of articles outlining the new publication's political positions, the first dealt with the Russian Social Democratic Labour Party (RSDLP) and quoted at length from a 1903 essay on the national question by Lenin, including his negative assessment of the PPS.[35] While Lenin supported the right of oppressed nations to self-determination (independence from colonial rule), even if they remained capitalist, he did not prioritise it over socialist revolution, especially if the bourgeoisie of the nation in question was not fighting for independence – as was the case at the time in Poland.[36] Having formed an alliance with the PPS, the PPSD and its newspaper *Naprzód* attacked the new journal and initiated what became known as the 'Grossman affair'. Grossman was threatened with expulsion, labelled a wrecker and accused of fraudulent fundraising activity. Grossman had been collecting, openly and transparently, contributions for the Committee for

Support of the Russian Revolution. He demanded a correction, which was rejected, and then an arbitration court to hear the charges he now levelled against the publication. Not only radical students, but also sections of the PPSD's own organization, mobilised in Grossman's support.[37]

Grossman got his wish but the party executive said he would be expelled if he did not resign from the editorship of *Zjednoczenie* within 48 hours. Losing his temper, Grossman refused.[38]

After expulsion, Grossman eventually quit *Zjednoczenie* and gained readmission to the PPSD. He did not want to cut himself off from its members, especially the Jewish workers he had won to the party's trade union activity through Ruch. By exposing the leadership to his criticisms and increasing his influence and support, however, the episode had served a political purpose. His name and politics were now 'known to every conscious Jewish proletarian in Krakow'.[39]

Building an independent Jewish party

The PPSD's reaction to criticism on the national question convinced Grossman of the need for independent Jewish representation within occupied Poland. He learned Yiddish to agitate among Jewish workers. Wary of his middle-class appearance, he approached them cautiously but without pretending to be something he was not. He would sit in cafes, talk to Jewish workers, win their trust and gently introduce them to the ideas of socialism. It was a slow process, but 12 members established a new general Jewish association, Postęp (Progress), in 1902. Out of this grew cultural groups and branches of the central social democratic unions.[40]

Dissatisfied by the PPSD's chauvinistic demands that Jews assimilate into 'higher' Polish culture, many Jewish members began to discuss forming an independent party. Towards the end of 1904, a secret Committee of Jewish Workers in Galicia agreed to make preparations for establishing an autonomous Jewish socialist party.

In January 1905, Grossman wrote and published a pamphlet in Polish, *The Proletariat and the Jewish Question*. Citing the example of the Bund, it argued that a Jewish social democratic party was the solution to the Jewish question *within* the labour movement.

Whereas Jews had suffered a common oppression in pre-capitalist societies, Grossman argued that there was no longer any Jewish question *in general*, but one for the Jewish bourgeoisie and another for the Jewish proletariat. It was therefore nonsensical to argue, as the PPSD did, that 'the solution to the Jewish question is a fair organisation of relations between Christian and Jewish communities'.[41] The bourgeois Jewish question, the oppression of the Jews as a distinct social group (regardless of class distinctions within it), 'is only a part of a general campaign in a class society, and the oppression of Jews is a part of a general oppression,' wrote Grossman. 'For the proletariat, the Jewish question in this sense has ceased to be an issue,' because class-conscious Jews knew that, while the struggle must be taken up now, it would only be resolved through socialism. 'The oppression of the Jewish proletariat as Jews will disappear when class society, of which it is a manifestation, also disappears. The victorious proletariat, having destroyed the class form of society, will abolish every oppression, as it removes the need for oppression and its tools!'[42]

Grossman clearly did not regard nations as permanent social phenomena, but he recognised that Jewish workers would remain a distinctive group under capitalism. The assimilationist position of the PPSD did not address the reality of everyday Jewish oppression.

The immediate issue was how to mobilise Jewish workers. At this stage, Grossman saw an independent party as a complementary extension of the General Austrian Social

Democratic Party (of which the PPSD was a member).

In contrast to the PPSD, Lenin regarded the autonomy accorded to constituent organisations of the Russian party as, 'providing the Jewish working class movement with all it needs: propaganda and agitation in Yiddish, its own literature and congresses, the right to advance separate demands to supplement a single general social democratic programme and to satisfy local needs and requirements arising out of the special features of Jewish life'.[43] But Lenin also accused the Bund of substituting the 'fig leaf' of federalism – which, he contended, would undermine the anti-Tsarist unity of the Russian Empire's working class for the policy of supporting the right to self-determination of oppressed nations, at a time when the bourgeoisie of oppressed nations had given up such a fight. For now, Grossman's position was more in line with the Bund and the Austrian party.

Initially, the enthusiasm of Jewish workers for their own party out-paced Grossman's strategic concerns, and he had to push back against calls for what he considered a premature break with the PPSD. The party was later launched at a secret meeting on May Day 1905. Its newspaper was *Yidisher Sotsial-Demokrat*, the *Jewish Social Democrat*.[44] The Jewish Social Democratic Party of Galicia (JSDP), explained one of its founders, Jakob Rose, to 2000 striking workers at its first meeting, arose 'not against the Polish or Ruthenian parties, but alongside them,' as demonstrated on the day by its collections for the PPSD's newspaper.[45]

Grossman was the principal author of *What Do We Want?*, the JSDP's manifesto. He wrote:

> It is necessary not only to speak to Jewish workers in a different language, one must also understand their psychology...An alien, Polish ideology...was forced upon

the Jewish masses and...the psychology of suffering was drummed into Jewish workers. Instead of arousing a sense of their own power and...worth as Jews, they were mournfully told: Jew, you're doomed; you will disappear. Instead of awakening their dignity everything was done to shake and weaken their dignity.[46]

Affiliation to the General Party, given its federalism and nationalism, was only desirable for practical reasons, to speak to the biggest possible audience and influence the most organised, conscious workers. JSDP leaders would have preferred a single cross-national Galician party.[47]

An appeal was made against the General Party's refusal to recognise the new party, with Grossman claiming the dispute was organisational, not political.[48] The appeal was interrupted by a working class uprising and the establishment of soviets (workers' councils)[49] in Russia, following the country's capitulation to Japan in February 1905. While the Austrian party did not match Russian social democracy's demands for a Republic or Constituent Assembly, it did begin a struggle for universal suffrage across the Austrian Empire. The JSDP 'put huge efforts' into supporting the organisation of a general strike. Grossman addressed large crowds and argued that in fighting for universal suffrage Jewish workers should also 'demand national autonomy, so that it will no longer be possible for the larger nations to overpower the smaller nations'.[50]

The Czech party called for another general strike for the end of 1905, but it was overruled by the General Party.[51] Suffrage was eventually granted in January 1907 for male workers aged 24 and over, the General Party having said that women would renounce their demand for the vote in the interests of a 'more effective' struggle.[52]

Despite the lack of recognition from the General Party, the JSDP had the open support of the Czech and Ukrainian parties;

and it would go on to attract more Jewish workers from the PPSD.[53]

In contrast to the right-wing of the social democratic movement, Grossman recognised throughout the campaign the real limitations of fighting for workers' power within the confines of bourgeois legality. Writing in a party report of the time, he notes:

[Working class] power is used in different ways. There were times when the proletariat fought, weapons in hand, on the barricades. Then weapons gave way to voting slips. Now we are preparing for a mass strike which is the start of an active revolutionary struggle...So we are not supporters of revolution for its own sake – but nor are we supporters of legality for its own sake. We regard barricades and voting slips as good in the same way. They are only means to our goal...The time is coming when we will again shake things up with the old revolutionary enthusiasm. The mass strike, the last step on the legal path is the first step of the revolution![54]

Grossman acknowledged that Galicia may be too undeveloped and agrarian for the working class to succeed. He pointed, however, to agrarian Russia, 'the classic land of the mass strike'.

The Proletariat and the Jewish Question had focused on organising within social democracy. The party now moved on to combatting antisemitism and national oppression in general. Like the Bund, Grossman argued that once democratised through the introduction of universal suffrage, parliament's competence in the area of national cultural affairs, essentially educational matters, should be passed to democratic national cultural institutions. He thought that, 'freed from national conflict, the central parliament will become a field of utterly unobscured class struggle'.[55]

While winning these rights was highly important, the latter

assessment proved too optimistic; as was his belief that the JSDP could begin to attract more middle-class members and field candidates in elections. Working class political activity began to die down as the economic upturn faded. The JSDP were put on the back foot as a result. Grossman himself was beaten up by the anti-socialist members of a fanatical Jewish religious sect. He took the offenders to court and won, a victory and a publicity coup for the JSDP.[56]

Bundism in Galicia and anti-Zionism

Another reason for starting an independent Jewish party had been the need to counter the influence of the Zionist movement, which advocated a settler-colonial solution to the Jewish question through the establishment of a mythical homeland, Israel, at the expense of Palestine and its Muslim-Arab majority population. In *Bundism in Galicia,* published in 1908, Grossman said that the PPSD's passivity over day-to-day Jewish struggles aided the Zionist cause. By invoking a solution in the distant future, whether in Palestine or under socialism, they both 'cut themselves off from the real context in which a solution to this question is necessary'.[57]

Grossman's earlier argument had focused on objective historical processes and political organisation characteristic of the orthodox Marxism of the Second International. He now came closer to Lenin's approach:

Recognition, based on scientific socialism, that all forms of social consciousness are to be explained in terms of class and group interests is of great practical significance in the assessment of a proletarian party...This is also significant to the extent that it is true in reverse, that is, the class interests of the proletariat find their expression in party consciousness (in the form of a programme); party consciousness is the multi-faceted expression of the proletariat's class interests and the most far-reaching interpretation of conclusions drawn from the objective trends of real social development. Workers' parties do not always fulfil this requirement (as evidenced by the PPSD). Both the character and the content of collective party thought remain *directly dependent on the particular party's adjustment to the very working class* whose expression it should be...The closest possible adaptation of the party organisation to the historical forms of the Jewish proletariat's condition...could only be achieved through the mutual organic growth of the party organisation and the workers' movement itself, just as the latter has grown out of capitalist society.[58]

Against the passive attitude of the PPSD, Grossman invoked Marx:

The words of the *Communist Manifesto* that '... the emancipation of the workers must be the act of the working class itself ...' mean, as far as the Jews are concerned, that their emancipation can only be the product of their own political struggle. And really, equal national rights for the Jewish proletariat are not at all an exotic blossom, ripening somewhere outside the sphere of the day-to-day struggle, that will somehow bring the Jews good fortune on the victory of socialism. Equal rights can only be the result of an inner development which includes both a subjective factor, i.e. the Jewish working class, and an objective factor, i.e. the rest of capitalist society. [59]

As Kuhn points out, James Connolly, leader of the 1916 Easter Rising, had expressed ideas about the liberation of Irish workers in 'remarkably similar terms'.[60]

Although Grossman's Bundist and federalist positions remained, the text represented a significant advance. His dialectical (two-sided) approach overcame the orthodoxy of the Second International, which one-sidedly focused on the future society, and paralleled the theory and practice that paid off for the Bolsheviks in the Russian Revolution. Clearly, those who would later dismiss Grossman as an economic determinist would have to ignore his early work as a party organiser.

Academia and statistical expertise

With the labour struggles of eastern Europe having petered out, at the end of 1908 Grossman moved to Vienna, capital of the Austro-Hungarian Empire. Although he remained a member of the JSDP executive (until 1911),[61] he concentrated on pursuing a career in law and academia. Whether he felt this would aid his political development or just wanted a break from politics is unclear. In December, he married Janina Reicher, an artist. They went on to have two children, Jean Henri and Stanislaus Eugen.

Attracting Grossman to Vienna were Carl Grünberg – the first Marxist to gain professorship at a German-speaking university – and the archives of the imperial capital. Grünberg was also Jewish and his scholarly research on Austria's eighteenth- and nineteenth-century economic history complemented Grossman's work on the political economy of the Jewish working class. With Grünberg's support and guidance, Grossman began to work on a major piece of research that would be the basis for a higher doctorate and hence a university post.

Grossman researched Austria's 'great epoch of reform' in the eighteenth century, particularly the impact of the Habsburg monarchs' trade policy of 1772-90. Through this work he developed expertise in statistics. He published a substantial paper in 1912, presented to the 5th Conference of Polish Economists, which evaluated and improved previous estimates of the size of the Polish territory occupied by Austria during the eighteenth century. In it he argued that the early Habsburgs pursued a then-progressive trade policy in economic development, in contrast to the backwards feudalism of the Polish Republic.[62] In a one-two blow to the conventional nationalist view that the Polish nobility had been a progressive force, he also argued that antisemitism had been the weakest flaw in Polish economic development, since the harsh fiscal burdens placed on Jewish merchants (wholesale traders) had stymied their pioneering contribution in the development of the putting-out system in textiles and other industries.

A comrade complained that 'the Kaiser's goodwill' had been Grossman's explanation for Austrian policies in Galicia. Grossman later insisted that – despite its lack of references to Marxism, for reasons of discretion – his study had been written from the standpoint of historical materialism (the method of analysing historical developments on the basis of interacting social forces; as opposed to idealism, i.e. man's developing consciousness):

> I show how Emperor Joseph II pursued the same goal as the French Revolution later on, namely the transition from a decentralised feudal state to a centralised capitalist regime. As the bourgeoisie was strong in France, the revolution was driven from below and the bourgeoisie achieved its goal. It was different in Austria. As the bourgeoisie was still weak, undeveloped, the goal which Joseph II pursued could only be achieved from above, with the help of the bureaucracy. This also explains why the project failed.[63]

World war and conscription

At the outbreak of World War I (WWI), Grossman was conscripted to the Austro-Hungarian army. In 1918, he was recruited as economic advisor to the foreign minister, Count Czernin, who negotiated the peace treaty with the Bolsheviks Leon Trotsky and Karl Radek at Brest-Litovsk.[64] Grossman even worked for the Austrian authorities during their brief occupation of the Polish city of Lublin.[65] There is no evidence that he returned to independent political work during this time or of whether he considered resisting conscription, which would have meant capital punishment. (His mother destroyed many of his documents for fear of police visits).[66]

After the war, mutinies and mass action brought down the monarchies in both Germany and Austria-Hungary, but the new parliamentary regimes remained committed to capitalism. In Germany, the ruling class deployed both carrot and stick to prevent revolution (see chapter 3).

In Austria, the right social democrat Otto Bauer became the foreign minister in a coalition government and played a significant role in persuading Austrian soviets that their interests lay with reformism.[67] Seeking to break the internationalism of these workers' councils, the coalition government denied citizenship to foreigners, primarily to prevent 35,000 Galician Jews, most of them refugees, from staying in Vienna. Social democratic ministers broached no serious opposition to this xenophobic, anti-semitic and anti-worker policy. Grossman, as Grünberg wrote, 'experienced the blow of being designated a Pole'.[68] In 1919 Grossman moved to Warsaw, capital of the second Polish Republic. He worked as a public servant in a senior role for the Polish Central Statistical Office (GUS). He would also return to active politics.[69]

Recovering crisis theory

On a visit to Krakow, Grossman delivered a lecture, 'The Theory of Economic Crisis', to the Academy of Sciences.[70] It marked the beginning of what became the central theme of his political and scholarly work. The short paper later published in 1922 argued that most economic theorists had relied too heavily on detailed empirical data to investigate whether or not capitalism was inherently crisis-prone.

Against this 'naive empiricism', he said, it was necessary to study 'logical constructions' that are 'independent of our thought'. He drew an analogy with physicists who abstracted from the effects of the air when investigating falling bodies. This was a defence of the scientific methodology deployed by Marx, who constructed a 'pure' version of capitalism in isolation, without either 'the disturbing influences of foreign markets' or classes which are neither industrial capitalists nor productive (commodity-producing) workers (since these two conceptually constitute the capital relation). Consumption, whether in foreign or domestic markets, is thereby removed from the initial equation.[71]

Grossman explains the problem with a simple equation: industrial producers invest an amount of real capital in the course of the year (machines, buildings, raw materials, etc.), indicated by c; plus their outlay on wages, v. Thus they obtain an annual produce of $P = c + v + p$, where p indicates an average amount of profit. Assuming $c = 4000$, $v = 1000$, $P = 6000$, then $p = 1000$. From the value of 6000, the capitalist has to deduct 4000 for the renewal of real capital (c), so that the total amount of the joint income remaining is 2000, of which 1000 goes to the workers (v), and 1000 to the employers (p). If the latter's consumption (k) = 600, then the remaining part of the profit – the coefficient of accumulation (m) – is 400, which is dedicated to the expansion of production (accumulation).

If m can be reinvested in production, the capitalist mechanism under investigation is in a period of boom; if not, it is in a period of stagnation. This is 'the kernel of the problem', Grossman says – capital accumulation is 'planless'.

Otto Bauer, following the reformist economist Mykhailo Tugan-Baranovsky, had proposed 'that if only the proportions laid down by the formula as to the distribution of accumulated capital were observed, accumulation could be infinitely prolonged without crises': rising wages and falling prices would lower demand (correcting underproduction); and falling wages and rising prices would automatically lower supply (correcting overproduction). Grossman objected to this view, pointing out that large companies often deliberately restrict production to raise prices and secure higher profits at the expense of smaller competitors. At the same time, they cut their outlay on wages, not only in periods of depression but also in the fullest phase of development.

Using the example of new ships that could carry more tonnage than older designs, Grossman points out that a new product that operates at a higher profit than one it replaces can cause the company making the old product to go bust. The old product can then be bought up at a lower price and therefore begin to operate at a profit again:

> The apparatus of production, instead of becoming restricted, has been enlarged. And the crisis, nevertheless, has passed! What has been restricted is – the value of the ships. The crisis, then, is not a restriction of the real apparatus of production, but a breakdown of the accepted system of prices and values, and its reorganisation on a new level.

Crisis could only be avoided if both the amount of capital invested and then the value created in the production process was sufficient. Disproportion is not the core problem since it 'is a constant and unavoidable phenomenon'.

This showed the importance of something that had been forgotten since Marx: that commodities cannot be treated only as exchange-values, products that are exchangeable for money; but also as use-values, products that are only bought and sold if they fulfil a need or want. This would become another central theme in Grossman's work (see chapters two and four).

The Communist Workers Party of Poland

In 1920, Grossman joined the Communist Workers Party of Poland (KPRP), formed at the end of 1918 when workers had built councils across the country's industrial centres. The party represented a merger of the SDKPiL and the PPS Left. The stunning success of the Bolsheviks in Russia now meant communist parties could be formed with the backing of a new, Third International. Members who had previously supported an independent Jewish party to counter national chauvinism could now join a cross-national party with more confidence.

The KPRP was never legally registered and operated semi-clandestinely, but Grossman was not deterred by the riskiness of membership.[72] Party members regarded Grossman as one of its 'three wise men'.[73]

In 1920, Pilsudski, now chancellor, ordered the invasion of the Soviet Ukraine. The Polish army seized the Ukrainian capital, Kiev, in May. Pilsudski also had 2000 communists imprisoned to secure the home front.[74] After Soviet troops mounted a successful counter-offensive, communists in Poland could no longer do any legal or even semi-legal political work. Once the Red Army liberated Kiev, it moved into undisputed Polish territory. Consistent with his position on the national question, this was justified by Lenin on the basis of both self-defence and the prioritisation of socialist revolution.

Poles of military age were conscripted. Grossman was posted to the Artillery School in Toruń. The Red Army was pushed back just before reaching the town in August. Grossman had already had his military responsibilities terminated 'because of suspicious behaviour and [was] thereafter under police surveillance'. He later said that he had assisted Soviet forces on a railway.[75]

Grossman left the GUS because, according to Grünberg, 'he was not prepared to accept the fudging of the census results in favour of the Polish majority and against the interests of minorities'.[76] Around 30-40% of Poland's population was not ethnically Polish. In several eastern provinces, Ukrainians and Belorussians were in the majority, something chauvinist Polish parties did not want to acknowledge.

The labour aristocracy

Grossman went to the Free University of Poland, where he was appointed to a full professorship in economic policy in 1922. He also joined the People's University (PU), which brought together workers, students, intellectuals and peasants, worked with trade unions and offered popular and specialist courses. Grossman was secretary and then the chair, until 1925.[77]

In a short article for KPRP journal *Kultura Robotnicza* (*Workers' Culture*), 'The Economic System of Karl Marx', Grossman's main political intervention was his explanation for the failure of the Second International. Like Marx and Lenin, he argued that a privileged layer of workers and intellectuals, a 'labour aristocracy', had disproportionate power within the workers' movement and little incentive to abolish capitalism. Opportunism and reformism within the leadership of unions and workers' parties was the natural outgrowth of this influence, with the aim of duping the mass of workers and hamstringing their organisation for power.

> In the second volume of *Capital*, Marx gives some consideration to the possibility of production and consumption within the capitalist system becoming permanently stable. [Rudolf] Hilferding, [Karl] Kautsky and Bauer rushed to answer: such equilibrium is not only possible, but the mechanisms of capitalism are such that they automatically tend to restore equilibrium in production if it is temporarily disrupted.[78]

This approach regressed Marxism 'to the level of pre-Marxist theory'. Combined with his 1919 paper, it was already clear that the relationship between crisis and revolution was at the centre of Grossman's thought.

Marxian economics is the only scientific theory which predicted processes that are now under way, analysed them and formulated the laws of their historical development, the process of the breakdown and collapse of the capitalist system. The opportunist literary attempts to distort Marxist theory, still being undertaken, must always fail when confronted with reality. [79]

Grossman believed that the posthumous publication of the third volume of *Capital* in 1894 had been a turning point for the understanding of Marx's work that had been missed or ignored by the second internationalists.

Simonde de Sismondi

In 1923, Grossman wrote a lecture on Simonde de Sismondi, an economist born in 1773 in Geneva, Switzerland.[80] Whereas Luxemburg had emphasised the differences between Marx and Sismondi in her work on political economy, Grossman identified the latter as the first to 'scientifically discover capitalism'. Marx had, in fact, inherited his methodology from Sismondi, who had moved economics on from the one-sided treatment of the classical school of Adam Smith and David Ricardo (see chapter 4). He did this by identifying the dual character of the production of commodities as exchange-values and use-values. Without the latter, his predecessors used abstractions that distorted rather than simplified capitalism. Grossman says Sismondi therefore expressed 'the germ' of what Marx called the commodity fetish, which obscures real social relations (such as the fact that workers create all exchange-value but keep less than they create).

Before Marx, political economists had taught that 'the free

market' produces harmonious equilibrium, fixing any problems caused by dips in demand through falling prices. Sismondi departed from this idea. In the real world, many producers increase production during a downturn to increase sales and raise absolute profits.

In political terms, Sismondi backed reform to improve the immediate situation of the working class but also saw the necessity of a superior, planned system. While he advocated the abolition of exchange-value, he did not, however, realise that this entailed the abolition of privately-owned production. Nevertheless, Grossman controversially labelled Sismondi a socialist, saying that his 'doctrine constitutes one of the most important sources for the genesis of the scientific economic theory of Karl Marx'.

Hyperinflation and exile

As a branch of the Moscow-based Communist International (Comintern), the KPRP adopted sensible changes in policy in 1922; including the United Front tactic of seeking joint action with reformist parties and trade unions, while retaining the right to publicly criticise them in order to expose their leaderships, to win over their memberships (as opposed to the purely reformist Popular Front tactic (see chapter 3), which opposes such a right). Aspects of the sectarian heritage of the SDKPiL were replaced by the Bolshevik position on oppressed nationalities. The party stopped calling for the collective operation of large rural estates, a position Lenin had regarded as ultraleft at this time given the need to mobilise the masses of poor peasants. The KPRP's influence grew, not only among peasants and ethnically Polish workers, but also among Jews, White Russians, Ukrainians and Germans.[81]

In 1923, hyperinflation struck Poland. Workers organised mass strikes to keep wages in line with rising prices. The KPRP, with its already limited resources, was further hindered during this period by arrests. Grossman himself was imprisoned five times (for 8 months on one occasion) between 1922 and 1925. After his comrades launched a well-publicised campaign that involved personal approaches to members of the government, Grossman was freed from prison on the condition that he would leave the country other than for 2 weeks annually to visit family. On 4 November, 1925, he arrived in Frankfurt am Main in Hesse, the largest state in Germany's federal Weimar Republic. Grünberg arranged a post for him at the Institute for Social Research (IfS). Even before then, Henryk and Janina's marriage had broken down as a result of his political activity.[82]

The Institute for Social Research

The IfS, also known as the Frankfurt School, was funded by a number of young intellectuals from well-to-do families who were interested in Marxism and sympathetic to revolution. Felix Weil, for example, son of a multimillionaire grain trader, had 'put himself, in full uniform, at the disposal of the Frankfurt Workers' and Soldiers' Council during the November Revolution of 1918'. Two others, Max Horkheimer and Friedrich Pollock, the sons of wealthy Jewish industrialists in southern Germany, witnessed the Soviet Republic in Munich 'from a rather dignified distance'. None of them ever joined a communist party. They had not had the same involvement in the movement as Grossman,[83] who, however, had lost none of his upper-class eccentricities along the way. According to a former associate of the Institute, he 'would come to deliver lectures in Frankfurt with white gloves and a cane'.[84]

After some initial harassment from the German state, Grossman was free to dedicate himself to writing and teaching Marxist theory, so long as he did not join the Communist Party of Germany (KPD). He spent most of his time until November 1926 writing 'The laws of development of "pure" and empirical capitalism', which he had begun 3 or 4 years earlier.[85] During the period to 1933, six interconnected publications on economics and revolution – a book (see next chapter) and five major articles (see chapter 4) – drew or built on this manuscript.

The book was *The Law of Accumulation and Breakdown of the Capitalist System (Being also a Theory of Crises)*. It remains Grossman's best-known work and attracted vastly more public attention during the 1920s and 1930s than any other publication by a member of the IfS.[86]

Chapter 2

The Law of Accumulation and Breakdown

The Law of Accumulation and Breakdown of the Capitalist System (Being also a Theory of Crisis) came out a few months before the 1929 Wall Street Crash, when share prices on the New York Stock Exchange halved – wiping out $25 billion, $300 billion in 2020 money – between the start of September and the end of October.[87] While reformists had been declaring that capitalism stood stronger than ever, Grossman had foreseen a major crisis brewing in the US that would ruin its European debtors.[88]

Lamenting 'a whole generation'[89] of Marxists, from reformist social democrats to revolutionary communists, Grossman argued that the 'unsatisfactory state of literature on Marx is ultimately rooted in the fact – which may sound strange to some – that until today no one has proposed any ideas at all, let alone any clear ideas, about Marx's method of investigation'. Instead, the focus had been on interpreting the conclusions of Marx's arguments, which were 'worthless divorced from an appreciation of the way in which they were established'.[90]

Grossman's work subjected Marx's method to a reconstruction 'for the first time', and presented a 'fundamentally new perspective' on the argument in *Capital*; drawing out the 'theory of breakdown' that 'forms the cornerstone of the system of Marx'. Such a theory had long been debated but 'no one has ever attempted a reconstruction or definition of its place in the system as a whole'.[91] Hitherto, Marxists had made the mistake of taking 'only secondary surface appearances that stem from the essence of capital accumulation as their primary basis'.[92] As Grossman says:

To be sure, Marx himself referred only to the breakdown and

not to the theory of breakdown, just as he did not write about a theory of value or a theory of wages, but only developed the laws of value and of wages. So if we are entitled to speak of a Marxist theory of value or theory of wages, we have as much right to speak of Marx's theory of breakdown.[93]

As in *The Proletariat and the Jewish Question* and his major study of Austrian trade policy, the shortcomings of predecessors demanded a somewhat one-sided response. Lenin called this approach 'bending the stick', whereby the case being made had to be overstated somewhat to get the point across. In the preface of *The Law of Accumulation*, Grossman made it clear that although the book would focus on the economic question, he did not believe politics played out as a completely automatic reflex of economics:

> Because I deliberately confine myself to describing only the economic presuppositions of the breakdown of capitalism in this study, let me dispel any suspicion of 'pure economism' from the start. It is unnecessary to waste paper over the connection between economics and politics; that there is a connection is obvious. However, while Marxists have written extensively on the political revolution, they have neglected to deal theoretically with the economic aspect of the question and have failed to appreciate the true content of Marx's theory of breakdown. My sole concern is to fill this gap in the Marxist tradition.[94]

The labour theory of value

To grasp the breakdown theory, we must firstly understand the labour theory of value, i.e., that: capital's exploitation of commodity-producing human labour is the sole source of *surplus value* (represented in our formula as s); exchange-value; and profit. This includes scientific and intellectual contributions and any handling or transportation of finished or near-finished commodities.

We must also understand that *constant capital* (*c*, the outlay on machinery and other material inputs, the value of which is constant) tends to grow relative to *variable capital* (*v*, the outlay on labour; i.e. (changeable) wages that go to the working class). For if variable capital alone returns new value but shrinks relative to constant capital, then it is clear that the share of the value-creating component in the *organic composition of capital* (constant capital plus variable capital, *c+v*) tends to shrink proportionally and historically towards zero.

That constant capital grows relative to variable capital is obvious – that the means of production (M) grows relative to living labour (L) is historical (i.e. necessarily ongoing), and therefore true of every mode of production. What needs to be shown is that under capitalism the process is governed by the law of value, i.e. the labour theory of value. A recent example from 2015 makes the trend clear:

> In 1960, the most profitable company in the US, then the world's biggest economy, was General Motors (GM). In money, GM made $7.6bn that year. It also employed 600,000 people. Today's most profitable company employs 92,600. So where 600,000 workers would once generate $7.6bn in profit, now 92,600 generate $89.9bn, an improvement in profitability per worker of 76.65 times. This is pure profit for the company's owners, after all workers have been paid. Capital isn't just winning against labour: there's no contest. If it were a boxing match, the referee would stop the fight.[95]

Human labour power is a unique commodity in that it produces *surplus value* – the amount of value that goes to the capitalist after his hired workers have created enough value for themselves and their dependents to live on, i.e. *necessary labour time.*

Surplus labour time is the time workers work beyond necessary labour time. Since the going rate for labour power is necessary labour time, surplus labour time is surplus value that goes to the capitalist, *realised* through the sale of the commodities that workers produce.

The price of labour power is determined, in the abstract (i.e. in general), like the price of any other commodity – *on average*, the cost of its production, i.e. necessary labour time. But if commodities are sold for the cost of their production, how does the capitalist make any profit? The capitalist purchases the worker's human labour power – the ability to work – but, *uniquely, always* ends up with more than he paid for that commodity. The wage obscures the fact that the capitalist has only paid for necessary labour time. Profit then is essentially *unpaid labour*. The wage in monetary terms obscures *exploitation*. Wage labour is *wage-slavery*.[96]

Since capitalism 'presents itself as an immense accumulation of commodities', says Marx, an analysis of capitalism must begin with the commodity.[97] What all commodities have in common is that they are all exchangeable – they all possess *exchange-value*. Moreover, as they are all products of labour, what they all have in common which gives them this exchange-value is *general* (as opposed to particular types of) human labour. The total value of all commodities, therefore, if they were to be added up, is determined by *total socially necessary labour time* – how much labour time they needed for their production.

When labour-saving technology reduces total labour time – per commodity, for an expansion in the total number of commodities may mean an absolute increase – there *tends* to be a *relative* fall in the surplus value contained in the total value of commodities, i.e. less surplus value per commodity. This is despite the fact that the rate of exploitation has increased, i.e. that each worker is now giving the capitalist more surplus labour time and therefore producing more surplus value relative to their necessary labour. Since there are fewer workers relative to the total amount of the now expanded machinery, however, the contribution of the value-producing component, variable capital, shrinks relative to constant capital. 'The fall in value reacts back on the commodities that are still on the market but which were produced under the older methods... These commodities are devalued,' says Grossman.[98]

The dual character of production

As in 1919, Grossman stressed something his contemporaries had overlooked, the dual character of the commodity: it is at once an object of use, holding *use-value*; and something that is produced for profit and exchanged for another thing, containing an *exchange-value*. Producing a useful object is a sensuous, material process, rich in qualitatively different production tasks, workplaces, and diverse tools and materials. As objects of exchange, conversely, commodities embody only specific quantities of abstract human labour; produced for profit in the form of *values* (measured in labour time in the abstract) and exchange-values (measured by the prices of production and market prices in monetary terms).

Grossman now elaborated on these two simultaneous processes more clearly, naming the production process as both a labour process *and* a *valorisation* process which reproduces and expands existing capital in order to accumulate further value. This re-centred Marx's focus on exploitation, the labour theory of value and the very real difference between how production and consumption are experienced.

The possibility of crisis itself originates in the contradictory nature of the commodity. In a dialectical (bidirectional/ interactional) 'unity of opposites', the more abundant a use-value becomes, relative to demand, the less exchange-value it contains. The capitalist produces goods in greater abundance, *yet is compelled to expand absolute production yet further to make up for his falling profit rate.*

Since different commodities contain different magnitudes of value and cannot be directly exchanged, the use of money as a means of payment proceeds logically from this contradiction. It is not the exchange of commodities which regulates the magnitude of their value, but the magnitude of their value which controls their exchange-value. Exchange-value is the only form in which the value of commodities can be expressed. Someone will buy a use-value because they need or want it, but only if they have enough money, without which profit goes unrealised. But to focus on this last, 'surface level' aspect, which appears after the commodity has been produced, results in a crisis theory based on 'underconsumption' (see below). A proper Marxist analysis has to come back to the mode or point of production – and the point of production is profit and accumulation. Grossman writes:

> The specific nature of capitalist commodity production shows itself in the fact that it is not simply a labour process in which products are created by the elements of production M and L. Rather the capitalistic form of commodity production is constructed dualistically – it is simultaneously a labour process for the creation of products and a valorisation process. The elements of production M and L figure not only in their natural form, but at the same time as values c and v respectively. They are used for the production of a sum of values, w, and indeed only on condition that over and above the used up value magnitudes c and v there is a surplus s (that is, $s = w-c+v$). The capitalist expansion of production, or accumulation of capital, is defined by the fact that the expansion of M relative to L occurs on the basis of the law of value; it takes the specific form of a constantly expanding capital c relative to the sum of wages v, such that both components of capital are necessarily valorised. It

follows that the reproduction process can only be continued and expanded further if the advanced, constantly growing capital $c+v$ can secure a profit, s. The problem can then be defined as follows – is a process of this sort possible in the long run?[99]

Imperfect valorisation

It may be easiest to think of the problem as follows. The purpose of commodity production is to convert surplus value extracted from living labour into capital; i.e., to valorise the worker's activity. Valorisation is not possible, though, unless a *sufficient* magnitude of surplus value is produced, over and above the existing value of capital. If insufficient surplus value is generated, it only reproduces a *part* of capital or fails to expand it. The remaining part becomes surplus to requirements and loses its value. Labour's efforts to improve society through scarcity-reduction go to waste because there is no profit to be made by the capitalist. Grossman therefore says that this 'overaccumulation of capital' results from 'imperfect valorisation'.[100]

Imperfect valorisation therefore explains the cyclical emergence of economic crises. The total investment in production tends to grow faster than the growth of profits returned, since constant capital grows relative to variable capital. The mass of capital continues to rise but at a declining rate. This is *expressed* in a falling rate of profit – the ratio between surplus value and total capital, $s:(c+v)$.[101] There is a lack of surplus value relative to the total capital invested – an underproduction of surplus value is at the same time an overaccumulation of capital. When returns fall too low or collapse, the incentive to invest disappears and businesses shrink or go bankrupt. When this happens on an economy-wide scale – because the *general* rate of profit falls – the economy, the size of its output and activity, contracts.

The breakdown tendency, as the fundamental tendency of capitalism, splits up into a series of apparently independent cycles which are only the form of its constant, periodic reassertion. Marx's theory of breakdown is thus the necessary basis and presupposition of his theory of crisis, because... crises are only the form in which the breakdown tendency is temporarily interrupted and restrained from realising itself completely.[102]

Restoring the accumulation process

Imperfect valorisation *compels* the capitalist class to restructure their business operations and, where possible, the system as a whole. 'This involves groping attempts at a complete rationalisation of all spheres of economic life.'[103] It includes:

1) increasing the production of surplus value by raising the rate of exploitation; by

(a) increasing the production of *absolute surplus value*; that is, increasing the number of exploited workers, the length of the working day and the intensity of work (limited by the number of hours in the day, the physical health and ability of workers; the effectiveness of workers' resistance in trade unions and political organisations);

(b) increasing the production of *relative surplus value*; that is, reducing the value of labour power by cheapening the production of commodities, especially through innovation; or, to put it another way, increasing surplus labour time and reducing necessary labour time (limited by the development of technology and the effectiveness of workers' resistance);

(c) driving the cost of labour below its value (also known as super-exploitation) through wage reductions (per worker and/or in absolute terms), sackings and redundancies, attacks on workers' rights and conditions, etc. (limited by the effectiveness of workers' resistance).

2) making more surplus value *available for* accumulation by redirecting portions of it from public spending (welfare, etc) to the 'private sector' (through state subsidies, tax cuts, etc.) including the privatisation of state assets and public services.

3) the sufficient devaluation and centralisation of currency and capital (both in terms of money and privately-owned production; i.e. into relatively fewer hands) so that the value of constant capital decreases relative to that of living labour.

The cycle, however, repeats itself. Surplus value is *converted into capital faster than it is produced* and so capital once again over-accumulates. The overall mass of capital is now even greater than before, and so an even greater magnitude of surplus value is required alongside an even greater devaluation and centralisation of capital.

Crisis is therefore inherent to the capitalist system. Debt rises not because of arbitrary overspending by governments, banks, companies or consumers, but to cover the lag in the realisation of profit and in order to *make up for the underproduction of surplus value*.

While reformists after Marx claimed that crises become weaker as the monopolisation of production shuts out competition, in reality they tend to worsen. As Marx says:

> The *real barrier* of capitalist production is *capital itself*. It is that capital and its self-expansion appear as the starting and the closing point, the motive and the purpose of production... Capitalist production constantly strives to overcome these immanent barriers, but it overcomes them only by means that

set up the barriers afresh and on a more powerful scale.[104]

Harmonism vs breakdown

Both reformist and revolutionary Marxists had taken up their own explanations for economic crises, based on different elements of Marx's work, addressing either the *disproportionality* of capitalist production or the *underconsumption* of commodities. Disproportionality theorists see crises as arising from disproportions in growth among individual spheres of industry; i.e. from 'unregulated production', meaning that regulated production could prevent capitalist crises. The likes of Bauer and Hilferding saw the centralisation of capital through the increased monopoly ownership of industry and banking as counter-measures to prevent crises or reduce their severity. Similarly, the emergence of new economic sectors created new markets to absorb products which had previously been unsaleable.

Underconsumption theories assert that crisis is caused by commodities going unpurchased and profit therefore unrealised. This could be because capitalists invest too little, either due to 'greedy' hoarding or a 'lack of confidence' regarding returns on investment (without answering why that hoarding or lack of confidence exists). Workers therefore go underpaid and are forced to survive on fewer commodities. The solution is usually reform, with the state redistributing wealth more 'fairly' or evenly in favour of the working class through higher wages, tax and spend policies, or perhaps even the nationalisation of some key industries.

A variation of the theory points to a saturation of domestic consumption, making the solution the export of commodities to 'non-capitalist' foreign markets – an option that, in the analysis of Kautsky[105] and Rosa Luxemburg, would increasingly run out as the whole world became industrialised and capitalist. This version preserves Marx's breakdown tendency but locates it not in the nature of the commodity or production, but in the markets in which commodities are sold.

Bauer, the most influential theorist in the Austrian Social Democratic Party, had a foot in both disproportionality and underconsumptionist camps. He saw the regulation of consumption through monopoly prices as sufficient to prevent or overcome crisis, but also thought that the system 'automatically [cancels out disproportions of] overproduction and underproduction' because accumulation adjusts to population growth.[106] He accepted that capitalist crisis could only be completely eliminated through planned socialism, but like Hilferding thought that banks would play an increasingly 'socialising role'[107] in making this possible, since money, according to their theory, originates in the act of exchange and the demand for it. From this it follows that banks set the money supply and play a role in controlling and regulating production levels. Hilferding claimed that '[nationalising] six large Berlin banks would mean taking possession of the most important spheres of large scale industry'. In 1927, he said he had 'repudiated every theory of economic breakdown'.[108]

In 1899, Eduard Bernstein of the SPD, known as the first Marxist 'revisionist',[109] wrote in his book *Evolutionary Socialism* that, 'If the triumph of socialism were truly an immanent economic necessity, then it would have to be grounded in a proof of [an] inevitable economic breakdown.'[110] Grossman agreed – but not with Bernstein's contention that such proof was fanciful.

All the disproportionality and underconsumptionist theories are concerned with the sphere of circulation or consumption rather than that of production. To get back to Marx, Grossman had to prove that capitalism's problems originate within the mode of production itself.

That capitalism needs to keep accumulating, like a bodybuilder addicted to muscle gain, is not in dispute. To put it another way: it is not possible to maintain the size of the capitalist economy as it is by choice. A system based on profit-making – receiving larger returns than the amounts invested – implies growth. A business that does not make enough profit does not attract investment, and so it contracts and dies. What is in dispute is whether capital *can* accumulate indefinitely, without recession – when apparently external factors, such as economic mismanagement, war or 'natural disasters', are not to blame – or if there is an eventual historical limit. This is where Grossman diverges from Hilferding, Bauer and their fellow social democrats, whom he called neo-harmonists for promoting the old bourgeois view that capital accumulates harmoniously, without any inherent interruption.

If capitalism can grow indefinitely without internal factors causing recessions, then it can accumulate without ever coming up against an upper limit, in which case there is no economic argument for socialism; or, it would itself eventually transition into socialism automatically through monopolisation and socialisation, negating Marx's revolutionary conclusions.

Bernstein dismissed breakdown theory as 'purely speculative'[111] on the basis that the living standards of the working class had risen significantly during the nineteenth century. Marx, though, had never denied that the living standards of the working class could rise under capitalism. Indeed, he pointed out that the factor exerting an upward pressure on real wages was the growing intensity of labour demanded by capital accumulation. His argument was that wages and living standards would re-deteriorate, not because of a theory of underconsumption, but because of the breakdown tendency. The economic crises that culminated in World War I – expressed in 1907 by the US's first *national* banking crisis – proved Bernstein wrong.

After his about-turn on the necessity of revolution to the socialist project, Kautsky claimed that 'a special theory of breakdown was never proposed by Marx and Engels'.[112] Instead, unlike earlier socialist thinkers, Marx and Engels had foreseen in the working class an 'increase in its training and organisation, its maturity and power'.[113] Only this, not economic crisis, would lead to socialism. In 1927 Kautsky asserted that it was 'no longer possible to maintain that the capitalist mode of production prepares its own downfall'.[114] He declared – 2 years before the Wall Street Crash – that 'capitalism stands today, from a purely economic point of view, stronger than ever'.[115]

Behind the cruel irony of history that made a fool of Kautsky lay a political impulse towards reformism that outlives him. If capitalism could go on forever, and the living standards of the working class therefore continued to rise, why would the working class risk a bloody conflict with the bourgeoisie?

Hilferding's view of finance capital drew similar conclusions, drawing similar refutation from the world of facts. Although the contradiction between industry and banking worked itself out through a fusion of the two into finance capital, within that relationship the increasing tendency is for industry – which continues to work towards integrating everything under one sphere – to dominate the banks, not vice-versa. As Grossman says:

> Industry becomes increasingly more independent of credit flow because it shifts to self-financing through depreciation and reserves. There is a tendency for the share of equity funds to increase at the expense of borrowed funds, or for the company to acquire its own assets in the banks...this is one of the reasons why banks have been turning to the stock exchange by way of investments.[116]

It is only in the early stage of capitalist development that the banks dominate, when industry relies on an outside supply of credit to build itself up.

The historical tendency of capital is not the creation of a central bank which dominates the whole economy through a general cartel, but industrial concentration and growing accumulation of capital leading to the final breakdown due to overaccumulation.[117]

Distortions of breakdown theory

The few Marxists who upheld a breakdown theory – most notably committed revolutionaries like Rosa Luxemburg and Nicolai Bukharin – failed to grasp the root cause of breakdown.

Luxemburg argued that breakdown stemmed from advanced capitalist countries increasingly running out of 'non-capitalist' markets to which they could sell their surplus commodities (including productive machinery). But if this were the case, capitalism 'suffers from an excess of surplus value',[118] an impossibility since capitalism 'is dominated by a blind, limitless thirst for surplus value' – it is the underproduction of surplus value which creates crises. Luxemburg did not base her analysis in the immanent laws of accumulation, shifting 'the crucial problem of capitalism from the sphere of production to that of circulation'.[119.]

The Bolshevik Nikolai Bukharin failed to provide 'a serious account...and simply ends up with nebulous phrase-mongering about [expanding] "contradictions"'.[120] Bukharin put the revolution in Russia down to the misery brought about by war, but could not explain what had brought the war about. Louis Boudin, a Russian-born US Marxist, 'correctly says that breakdown can be understood and explained with the help of Marx's theory of value' but 'offers no proof' and therefore 'it is not surprising that he falls back' on Luxemburg's theory.[121]

It fell to Grossman then, on the eve of the Wall Street Crash, to clarify Marx's breakdown theory and to prove its validity.

The three stages of Marx's method

Marx's method, the method of *successive approximation*, consists of three stages: an abstract (simplified) reproduction scheme as a tool of theoretical analysis, generating a mathematical pattern for the growth of capital and the profit returned to it; hypothetical, simplifying assumptions which form its basis; and subsequent corrections to the scheme, whereby the assumptions are lifted, one by one, in order to move back from abstraction to empirical reality, as a process of verification.

This method is necessary since if the essence or inner structure of something could be known from its appearance, science would be superfluous. It was the ignorance, wilful or otherwise, of so many theorists of this basic methodological approach that caused them to misinterpret and distort Marx's findings. 'Provisional conclusions were taken for final results.'[122]

The scheme begins with *simple reproduction*, as if investment did not expand but simply preserved its own value. This works as an analytical mechanism because reproduction must renew itself before it can expand, i.e. it includes simple reproduction. Marx here assumes that: commodities sell at prices directly proportional to their labour values; there is no change in the methods of production, the organic composition of capital, the rate of surplus value or the rate of profit; there are only two classes: the industrial capitalists and the productive workers. In the third volume of *Capital* he lifts these assumptions.

In his first chapter, Grossman repeats Marx's method but uses Bauer's (1913) scheme, since it had been cited as proof of harmonious accumulation. Bauer's scheme featured a rising organic composition of capital, something Marx had not got round to including in such a scheme before his death. The ratio Bauer used for his starting organic composition, of $c{:}v$ being only 2:1, was not especially realistic, but Grossman stuck with it so as to expose Bauer's conclusions.

In Bauer's scheme, constant capital starts at 200,000;

variable capital at 100,000. The former is divided up: 120,000 in Department I (means of production); 80,000 in Department II (means of consumption, i.e. consumer goods). Variable capital is split evenly, 50,000 in each. The constant capital grows at 10% a year and variable capital at 5%. The rate of surplus value is constant, at 100% (surplus labour time matches necessary labour time). Although capitalist consumption (k) increases absolutely, increases in both productivity and the mass of surplus value allow a progressively greater portion of the surplus value to be earmarked for accumulation; both departments annually dedicate the same percentage. The rate of profit tends to fall.[123]

Proceeding from his assumptions, Bauer believes his scheme shows that capital accumulates indefinitely so long as the output of exchange-values from the two departments is kept in the correct ratios. The portion of surplus value reserved for the consumption of the capitalists represents a continuously declining percentage of surplus value, but it grows absolutely, thereby providing the motive that drives capitalists to expand production.[124] Grossman says:

> We might imagine that Bauer's harmonist conclusions are confirmed. The percentage fall in the rate of profit is of no concern because the absolute mass of profit can and does grow as long as the total capital expands more rapidly than the rate of profit falls...Is the falling rate of profit a real threat to capitalism? Bauer's scheme appears to show the opposite.[125]

And yet, precisely using Bauer's scheme, Grossman shows that Bauer's conclusions represent a 'banal delusion'.[126] Bauer only runs the scheme through four cycles or years of reproduction. 'If Bauer had followed through the development of his system over a sufficiently long time-span he would have found, soon enough, that his system necessarily breaks down.'[127]

Following the scheme through to year 36, the portion of surplus value reserved for capitalist consumption 'can only expand up to a definite high point. After this it must necessarily decline because it is swallowed up by the portion of surplus value required for [accumulation].'[128] A higher starting ratio of c to v would have revealed this sooner.

	c	v	s	accumulation	k
Commencement	200	100	100	20+ 5= 25	75
After 20 years	1222	253	253	122+13=135	118
After 30 years	3170	412	412	317+21=338	74
After 34 years	4641	500	500	464+25=489	11
After 35 years	5106	525	525	510+26=536	-11

Bauer's reproduction scheme taken to year 35. Here, Grossman has merged the departments (the separated version is not included in the abridged version) in order to make Bauer's schema more realistic, since without competition the rate of profit would vary from sphere to sphere. Competition has the effect of equalising rates of profit, which in turn cause production prices to deviate from values (see chapter four).[129]

Grossman explains that accumulated surplus value must be divided into three corresponding fractions: additional constant capital (more materials, tools, machinery, etc; a_c); additional variable capital (more labour to work the new inputs; a_v); and a consumption fund for the capitalists (k).

If the available surplus value could cover only the first two, accumulation would be impossible. For the question necessarily arises – why do capitalists accumulate? To provide additional employment to workers? From the point of view of capitalists that would make no sense once they themselves get nothing out of employing more workers.[130]

Despite the falling rate of profit, accumulation accelerates because the scope of accumulation expands not in proportion to the level of profitability, but in proportion to the base of the already accumulated capital.

In year 11, the capital value has expanded to 681,243, or by 227%, despite a continuous fall in the rate of profit. In the second decade the rate of capital expansion amounts to 236%, although the rate of profit falls even further, from 24.7% to 16.4%. In the third decade accumulation proceeds still faster, with an increase over 10 years of 243%, when the rate of profit is even lower. Bauer's scheme shows a declining rate of profit coupled with increasing accumulation. The constant capital grows from 50% of the total product in the first year to 82.9% of the annual product by year 35. Capitalist consumption (k) reaches a peak in year 20, then declines both relatively and absolutely and then finally disappears in year 35.

It follows that the system must break down. The capitalist class has nothing left for its own personal consumption because all existing means of subsistence have to be devoted to accumulation.[131]

In year 35 variable capital reaches a value of 540,075, but on Bauer's assumption of a 5% increase in population, 551,584 is required. There is a deficit of 11,509 on the accumulated variable capital, without which the system cannot be reproduced for a further year.

Bauer's assumptions cannot be sustained any further, the system breaks down. From year 35 on any further accumulation of capital under the conditions postulated would be quite meaningless. The capitalist would be wasting effort over the management of a productive system whose fruits are entirely absorbed by the share of workers. If this state persisted it would mean a destruction of the capitalist mechanism, its economic end. For the class of entrepreneurs, accumulation would not only be meaningless, it would be objectively impossible because the overaccumulated capital would lie idle, would not be able to function, would fail to yield any profits. (Marx): 'There would be a steep and sudden fall in the general rate of profit.'[132]

Profitability depends on the relationship between the rate in the increase of profit and the magnitude of capital. Overaccumulation is 'inevitable':[133]

The other side of the accumulation process

Grossman then stresses the importance of the other side of the accumulation process – that alongside unemployed capital grows unemployed labour – since this could only be assessed by extending Bauer's scheme beyond the sunlit uplands of its first 4 years.

Overaccumulation means that capital 'grows faster than the surplus value extortable from the given population, or that the working population is too small in relation to the swollen capital'. Accumulation is insufficient to absorb the annual increase in population. Thus in year 35 the rate of accumulation requires a level of 510,563 a_c + 26,265 a_v = 536,828. But the available mass of surplus value totals only 525,319. The rate of accumulation required to sustain the scheme is 104.6% of the available surplus value, 'a logical contradiction and impossible in reality…The extension of Bauer's scheme shows that in year 35 there are 11,509 unemployed workers who form a reserve army.' In addition, because only a part of the working population now enters the process of production, only a part of the additional constant capital ($510,563\, a_c$) is required for buying means of production. The active population of 540,075 requires a total constant capital of 5,499,015; the result is that 117,185 represents a surplus capital with no investment possibilities.[134]

With the consumption fund of the capitalists shrinking, they are bound to make efforts to reverse this trend. They must either cut their expenditure on wages,

> or cease to observe the conditions postulated for accumulation, that is, the condition that constant capital must expand by 10% annually to absorb the annual increase in the working population at the given technological level. This would mean that from now on accumulation would proceed at a slower rate, say 9.5% or 8%...and to an increasing degree. In that case accumulation would fail to keep step with the growth of the population.[135]

The installation of new machinery slows down and a growing reserve army of labour forms, even if wages are assumed to remain constant.

Other variations in the scheme show that the breakdown tendency can be pushed back or forward. For example, if variable capital grows, due to wage rises, and the population stays the same, the breakdown tendency speeds up; but if it rises as a result of a rise in the population, it is held back because more workers are contributing to the production of surplus value.

The third stage of Marx's method

Bauer did not explore any kind of successive approximation. He treated his simplifications as representative of empirical reality. Grossman was more thorough. Having found that Bauer's 'pure' form of capitalism broke down in the long run, he now had to verify this law and see if this remained the case when the factors left out for the purpose of simplification were reintroduced. Do they help or hinder valorisation? Do any of them suppress the breakdown tendency altogether?

There is a logical shortcut to the answer: for any counter-tendencies that emerge *spring from the primary tendency*. The breakdown tendency and the counter-tendencies are *part of the same piece of elastic*. Capitalism is a total system and has to be understood in its totality. By lifting and varying the simplifications, Grossman shows that Marx's theory works at different levels of abstraction, providing the clarity that exposes justifications for reformism.

We will run through some of the main counter-tendencies to prove the point, but as a rule: the breakdown tendency is strengthened by a higher organic composition of capital and a faster rate of accumulation of constant capital; and weakened by a higher rate of surplus value.

Devaluation and credit

Innovations demanded by accumulation devalue labour power, commodities and capital, so the assumption of constant values cannot be maintained. The quantity of surplus value is calculated against a reduced capital value. The rate of valorisation rises and delays the breakdown tendency.

> However much devaluation of capital may devastate the individual capitalist in periods of crisis, they are a safety valve for the capitalist class as a whole. For the system, devaluation of capital is a means of prolonging its life span, of defusing the dangers that threaten to explode the entire mechanism. The individual is thus sacrificed in the interest of the species.[136]

But since the share of the value-creating variable capital shrinks, the same tendency that has staved off breakdown goes on to reproduce it. 'A capital that fails to fulfil its function of valorisation ceases to be capital; hence its devaluation.'[137]

Fixed capital

Fixed capital is the fixed component of constant capital: machinery. (The non-fixed part comprises circulating capital, i.e. wages, raw materials, rents, etc.) In the assumed scheme, the life cycle of fixed capital equals one period of reproduction. Realistically, fixed capital operates over several cycles. 'In this case even if the value of the fixed capital is transferred to the product in a smaller annual rate of depreciation, it nevertheless helps in creating a growing mass of value, and therefore of surplus value, in proportion to its actual durability.'[138] Technological improvements that progressively consolidate the physical durability of fixed capital strengthen this factor.

For the same reason, however, the rate of 'moral depreciation' also increases. Fixed capital, despite its improved durability, is replaced more frequently; and so, through disuse, loses its use-value and exchange-value in less and less time, long before expiring physically.

Prices, competition and centralisation

Since value is created only by labour, price rises have no impact on the absolute mass of profit. They can only play a role in centralising existing value. Most innovations and expansions are made when prices have fallen, allowing some capitalists to buy new inputs for a song and paving the way for an economic upturn, even without updating technical methods. A portion of the unemployed are reabsorbed back into work, boosting the base for both surplus value production and the realisation of profit. If prices do not fall then production only continues on the existing scale. The capitalist has a surplus of goods – at some point they are bound to reduce prices to give the goods a better chance of selling. Competition intensifies.

Until now, the capitalist class has been treated as a single entity. To understand the changes to the price and centralisation of capital, competition must be reintroduced: 'A capitalist working with improved but not as yet generally adopted methods of production sells below the market price, but above his individual price of production; his rate of profit rises until competition levels it out,'[139] says Marx. The fight over profits becomes a fight to minimise losses, to pass them on to a rival. 'For the class as a whole, the loss is unavoidable. But how much each individual member has to bear, now becomes a question of strength and cunning, and competition then becomes a struggle between hostile brothers.'[140]

Competition itself thus compels mergers. Two individual capitals can only outcompete a third and fourth rival by combining forces. The new enterprise has a higher rate of productivity. The elements of variable capital are cheapened and the rate of surplus value increases. Surviving rivals are forced to follow suit. Like cadavers pillaged by vultures, those who go bust have their depreciated capital bought up on the cheap, furthering centralisation.

The rise of ever-greater monopolies is therefore inevitable. In 1975, the biggest 100 public companies in the US took in about 49% of the earnings of all US public companies; in 2015 the figure had risen to 84%.[141] A 2011 study found that, of 43,000 international corporations based in 116 countries, 40% of them were owned or controlled by just 0.5% of the world's biggest companies.[142]

As smaller competitors have been swallowed up by monopolies, over half of all firms have disappeared over the past 20 years. The smaller capitalists usually remain in denial: 'On this trend, by 2070 we will only have one company per industry,' write the authors of *The Myth of Capitalism: Monopolies and the*

Death of Competition.[143] 'The scale of mergers is so extreme, you would almost think American capitalists were trying to prove Karl Marx right.'[144]

Capital renewal

There is an opposing, albeit weaker, tendency to the increasing concentration of capital. A continual penetration by capital into new spheres means portions of the original capitals break off and function independently. Because the minimum amount of capital required to sustain larger enterprises is very high, smaller capitals have more leeway to experiment and innovate. They have a lower organic composition, produce new use-values and create new investment opportunities. The organic composition later rises, however, and/or the business merges with another.

The reserve army of labour

Once Bauer's scheme is extended, the development of a reserve army of labour is shown to become inevitable. Labour is abundant and therefore cheap. The unemployed exert a downward pressure on the level of wages so that they fall below the value of labour power (because the threat of unemployment and the availability of replacements compels those who are employed to accept lower wages). This partially transforms necessary labour time into surplus labour time. Far from underconsumption producing the crisis, depressing the cost of labour power helps to solve it, exposing 'the complete superficiality of those theoreticians in the trade unions who argue for wage increases as a means of surmounting the crisis,' says Grossman.[145]

At the same time as depressing wages, capital has created a problem for itself by shrinking the valorisation base.

Circulation

Annual reproduction is unrealistic. Production time is continually speeding up, while turnover time (the rate at which inventory or assets sell or exceed their useful life) varies from one branch of industry to another. Better productivity in turn speeds up the circulation of capital through improved transportation and communications. A £10m investment returning £11m is a 10% rate of return, but becomes 20% if the return can be achieved in 6 months instead of 12. A greater amount of surplus value is available sooner, and the portion of capital that has to remain in circulation is reduced, meaning more can be dedicated to productive capital. Storage costs can also be reduced (hence the contemporary 'just in time' system).

More surplus value is produced in less time, but there is an average fall in value in relative terms per commodity. The law of value giveth and taketh away.

Rents and levies

Some of the reintroduced factors outright assist the breakdown tendency. Landlords, for instance, eat into the profits of industrial capitalists by charging them ground rent (a clear source of division in the ruling class).

Commercial rent has a similar impact to ground rent (as do other levies and interest). This inspires a struggle against intermediary traders; they are absorbed and rationed by merged enterprises. Commercial agents cannot be completely done away with, however, as they fulfil necessary roles in the process of circulating industrial capital. Their role reaches a maximum under capitalism with the full development of commodity production.[146]

The middle stratum of commercial wage-workers – such as those involved in marketing, logistics or middle management – increases the outlay of the industrial capitalist without directly increasing surplus value. They are unproductive; their consumption reduces the fund available for the employment of productive workers.

'Third persons' and consumers

Other 'third persons', such as bureaucrats and the professional stratum, have the same effect. There is overlap with consumers as a whole. Grossman explains:

> Of course these groups perform various services in return, but the non-material character of such services makes it impossible for them to be used for the accumulation of capital. The physical nature of the commodity is a necessary precondition of its accumulation. Values enter the circulation of commodities, and thereby represent an accumulation of capital, only insofar as they acquire a materialised form.
>
> Because the services of third persons are of a non-material character, they contribute nothing to the accumulation of capital. However, their consumption reduces the accumulation fund. The larger this class the greater the deduction from the fund for accumulation.

Grossman noted that in Britain, 'where there is a large number of such persons, the tempo of accumulation will have to be slower'. Nearly a century on, Britain probably has the lowest rate of profit in the world.[147] As the oldest capitalist superpower, with perhaps the highest organic composition of capital, this makes perfect sense. Only in this context can the 'Brexit' crisis (Britain's departure from the European Union (EU)) be properly understood. Around 80% of Britain's domestic economic activity is now in services. Services workers produce new value if they are employed by capital (as opposed to a customer) but only if they handle finished or near-finished commodities. They are therefore not as productive as manufacturing workers.

Of course, Britain's wealth is largely a legacy of its former empire. Yet this small island remains the sixth richest country in the world. While the rate of surplus value production is higher in the most developed countries, because of their higher technological base, they are also dependent on what may be the most important counter-tendency.

Imperialism and war

Towards the end of the nineteenth century, capitalism began to pass from the era of the 'free market' or 'competitive capitalism' into what Lenin, writing in 1916, called its 'highest stage' – imperialism, or monopoly capitalism, effectively a fusion of banking and industrial capital. Corporations emerged owning almost the entirety of branches of industry or even combinations of them.

The 'primitive accumulation' of the colonial powers through direct plunder and enslavement enabled their industrialisation and the efficiencies of mass production; creating dominant large-scale enterprises, and specialised and standardised production, making Britain the 'workshop of the world'. British capitalism, however, came up against the limits of its working population. British capitalists were compelled to export their surplus capital to expand the exploitable labour base and provide an outlet for investment by beginning to industrialise their colonies. Slavery in the colonies became a fetter on capital because it is a form of constant capital and humans cannot work as fast as machines.

Around the 1870s, exporting means of production and loan money started to become more profitable than exporting means of consumption. The former took advantage of a lower organic composition of capital and a higher rate of exploitation, meaning the latter could be imported at a cheaper price than if they were produced and consumed domestically. Capital exports were increasingly needed to push back the breakdown tendency.

Today, Britain is the most parasitic imperialist power, exporting capital equitable to 560% of its GDP in 2015.[148] According to a 2016 War on Want report, for example, 101 companies listed on the London Stock Exchange controlled more than $1 trillion in mining and energy resources in 37 Sub-

Saharan African countries.[149] Much of the value created by the workers they employ is funnelled back into the City of London, Britain's parasitic financial centre. In bulk, Britain's capital outflows come second only to those of the US, which became the dominant world power after World War II (WWII) partly because the fighting had not taken place on its turf but also because Britain had to hand over large parts of its empire to the US in return for the US's help in defeating Nazi Germany. The US's enormous and integrated industrial base gave it huge advantages over Europe anyway, and its currency had been left intact, meaning the US dollar could take over from British pound sterling as the world's reserve currency. In response, France and Germany have taken steps to form a European imperialist bloc – through the EU and eurozone – that can compete with the US, while Japan has long been the weakest of the traditional imperialist nations.[150]

Foreign trade in general expands the base of productive workers and the multiplicity of use-values, reduces costs through efficiency gains, and relatively increases the speed of circulation. Furthermore, because profit rates tend to average out across branches of industry on the world market (a higher rate falls to the average once the attraction of investment saturates and competitors catch up), the commodities from the advanced country, with the higher organic composition, will be sold at prices of production higher than their value; and vice-versa. Surplus value is 'transferred from the less developed to the more developed capitalist countries because its distribution is determined not by the number of workers employed in each country but by the size of the functioning capital,' says Grossman. He called this 'unequal exchange', a term that became fashionable in the 1970s.[151]

This economic and social relation continues today. According to one study, between 1980 and 2012 the net outflow of value from 'developing and emerging' countries into 'developed' nations totalled $16.3 trillion;[152] a significant slice given that the size of the world economy in 2012 was $75 trillion.

'Such transfers become a matter of life and death for capitalism,' says Grossman, because at advanced stages of accumulation, 'it becomes more and more difficult to valorise the enormously accumulated capital.'[153] This explains the increasing aggression of imperialist 'foreign policy' – the imperialist destruction of Afghanistan, Iraq, Libya, Syria and so on, just recently.[154]

It is important to stress that imperialism developed in order to counter the breakdown tendency. Even Lenin's revered pamphlet *Imperialism: The Highest Stage of Capitalism* comes in for stick from Grossman. Although 'he makes many acute observations',[155] Lenin

linked [the tendency of stagnation and decay] to the growth of monopolies. That there is such a connection is indisputable, but a mere statement is not enough. One is not dealing simply with the phenomena of stagnation…Imperialism is characterised by both stagnation and aggressiveness. These tendencies have to be explained in their unity…In fact both phenomena are ultimately rooted in the tendency towards breakdown…The growth of monopolisation is a means of enhancing profitability by raising prices and, in this sense, is only a surface appearance whose inner structure is insufficient valorisation.[156]

Grossman argued that, while capital exports had previously characterised the slump stage of a country's economic cycle, they grew enormously and became more or less constant around 1900. He therefore agreed with Lenin's characterisation of imperialism as a qualitatively new development, but one that emerged from the intensification of an existing trend.

Eugen Varga, the chief economic advisor to Joseph Stalin,

Lenin's successor in the Communist Party of the Soviet Union (CPSU), denied the possibility of a saturation of capital in any single country, simply saying that higher rates of profit were the attraction for capital exports.[157] In a brave and devastating critique of Varga – given Varga's closeness to Stalin – Grossman pointed out that this flatly contradicted the law of value:

> [T]o suppose that capital can expand without limits is to suppose that surplus value can likewise expand without limits, and thus independently of the size of the working population. This [would mean] that surplus value does not depend on labour.[158]

While imperialism is necessary to stave off breakdown, it also has the opposite effect in those countries exploited by it and frozen out of its monopolies on raw materials. Since imperialism leeches off of those countries, the repercussions are felt 'at home' both economically and politically.

One of its clearest effects is found in imperialist competition, where the oppressor countries are drawn into violent conflict with each other over resources that are often half the world away:

> With the progress of accumulation the number of countries grows in which accumulation approaches absolute limits. In proportion to the growth in the number of countries which export capital, competition and the struggle for profitable outlets is bound to intensify. The repercussions of this will necessarily sharpen the crisis at home. If the early crises of capitalism could already lead to wild outbreaks, we can imagine what crises will be like under the growing weight of accumulation when the capital exporting countries are compelled to wage the sharpest struggles for investment outlets on the world market.[159]

Capitalism's decaying nature led to imperialism and – via further breakdown – intensifying imperialist rivalry and war, a much more satisfactory explanation than Kautsky's belief that war is driven merely by 'uncivilised' ruling classes.

At the same time, the destruction of war is the ultimate means of devaluing capital and labour power. War is therefore caused by and a temporary solution to the breakdown tendency. It 'wards off imminent collapse' and 'creates a breathing space' for accumulation.[160] Although military expenditure itself is an unproductive drain on capital, innovations paid for by the state are later privatised along with the profits. The tribute collected by the victors of war also further centralises capital.

Eventually, however, all of the counter-tendencies must exhaust themselves.

Despite the periodic interruptions that repeatedly defuse the tendency towards breakdown, the mechanism as a whole tends relentlessly towards its final end with the general process of accumulation. As the accumulation of capital grows absolutely, the valorisation of this expanded capital becomes progressively more difficult. Once these counter-tendencies are themselves defused or simply cease to operate, the breakdown tendency gains the upper hand and asserts itself in the absolute form as the final crisis.[161]

Revolutionary conclusions

In the final chapter, Grossman draws his conclusions: the breakdown tendency periodically forces the capitalists to attack the wages and conditions of the working class – and eventually becomes so strong that the latter is driven to revolution. Because capital does not accumulate harmoniously, there can be no seamless or reformist transition to socialism. Grossman's economic study therefore provides a sound justification for the revolutionary position of Marx and Lenin.

The accumulation process itself entails a class struggle over allocations of surplus value, since the capitalist can only sustain their consumption by taking a larger share from the working class. Real wages may rise for a while but inevitably decline.

The past 40 years have borne this trend out. US labour's net productivity increased by 108.1% in 1948-79, and wages nearly kept up, growing by 93.2%. In 1979-2018, by contrast, the figures were 69.6% and 11.6%.[162] This second period began with the onset of 'neoliberalism', when Ronald Reagan's Republican administration set about rolling back the postwar gains of social democracy, or 'Keynesianism', including a minimal nationalisation programme, which had been necessary to placate a rebellious working class and because the private sector could not afford the enormous postwar rebuilding costs. Far from being a step on the way to socialism, social democracy merely paved the way for the onslaught of neoliberalism, which attacked wages, deregulated banking and trade and reprivatised nationalised assets (at home and, via a series of violent coups, abroad). US labour's share of national income fell from 68% in 1980 to 62% in 2018. Conversely, corporate profits as a share of national income rose from 9% to above 13%.[163] This is despite the relatively greater growth of workers compared to capitalists, who were already in the minority.[164] Far from bringing about the prosperous home-owning democracies neoliberals initially promised, capitalism has instead produced its own grave-diggers:

If the largest and most important force of production, human labour power, is thus excluded from the fruits of civilised progress, it is at the same time demonstrated that we are approaching ever closer the situation which Marx and [Friedrich] Engels already foresaw in the *Communist Manifesto*: 'the bourgeoisie is unfit to rule because it is incompetent to assure an existence to its slaves within their slavery'. This is also the reason why wage-slaves must necessarily rise against the system of wage-slavery.[165]

Hilferding and others argued that the theory of breakdown should be rejected because it meant the working class should fatalistically await the mechanical demise of capitalism. Grossman saw things in a more nuanced, dialectical way, since working class resistance can deepen or bring about crises sooner.

Every major economic struggle necessarily becomes a question of the existence of capitalism, a *question of political power*. (Note the English miners' struggle, 1926.)

The struggle of the working class over everyday demands is thus bound up with its struggle over the final goal. The final goal for which the working class fights is not an ideal brought into the workers' movement 'from outside' by speculative means, whose realisation, independent of the struggles of the present, is reserved for the distant future. It is, on the contrary, as the law of capitalism's breakdown presented here shows, a result of immediate everyday struggles and its realisation can be accelerated by these struggles.

He had made a similar point in *Bundism in Galicia*, when he rejected the reformist separation of the final goal from the everyday struggles of Jewish workers.

Grossman also took on Hilferding's evolutionary theory. Although monopolisation certainly lays a basis for a 'final merger', a public monopoly, it does not mean capitalism can eliminate competition and thus conflict.

The more free competition is replaced by monopoly organisation on the domestic market, the more competition sharpens on the world market. If a river's flow is artificially blocked with a dam on one side of the stream, it presses on with even less restraint on the side that is still open.[166]

Grossman ultimately attributed capitalism's breakdown tendency to the contradiction between capitalist production as a labour process and as a valorisation process – a contradiction that his work had shown to be unsustainable:

> As a consequence of this fundamentally dual structure, capitalist production is characterised by insoluble conflicts. Irremediable systemic convulsions necessarily arise from this dual character, from the immanent contradiction between value and use-value, between profitability and productivity, between limited possibilities for valorisation and the unlimited development of the productive forces. This necessarily leads to overaccumulation and insufficient valorisation, therefore to breakdown, to a final catastrophe for the entire system.[167]

Liberated from the profit necessity, Grossman argued, production could be organised on a social basis as a technical labour process, without crises or the mystification of commodity fetishism:

> Where the social interrelations among individual production processes are immediately present and planned, there is no room for the law of value, whose most important task consists in the production of these social interrelations. Social equilibrium, calculated in advance, no longer has to be restored subsequently by means of the mystical veil of value.[168]

Defending the book

Anticipating criticisms within the book's pages did not stop them from coming. After quickly attracting widespread attention in the German-speaking world, both social democrats and communists accused Grossman of having a 'mechanical' conception of collapse and revolution. This despite his two-sided method of moving from pure to empirical capitalism; thorough assessment of modifying counter-tendencies; and pointed emphasis on class struggle and political power.

Grossman's most substantial defences initially came in letters and unpublished drafts, refuting the assertions of social democrats Julius Braunthal and Helene Bauer that the devaluation of capital overcomes the breakdown tendency rather than only weakening it temporarily. Countering this criticism made for elementary work, for their critique 'necessarily entails the proposition that there is no development of an ever-higher organic composition of capital in contemporary capitalist society!'[169]

Pointing to empirical examples, Grossman reasserted the fact that the absolute value of the mass of constant capital tends to more than offset devaluations. He also re-demonstrated the importance of treating commodities as use-values:

> In addition, when one does not start with the individual commodity but considers the total mass of commodities, devaluation has indifferent consequences...
>
> Let us assume that the entire rural economy uses 1,000 electric ploughs (each with a value of £80=£80,000) which are sufficient to work the available land. If productivity now doubles, so that with the same labour 2,000 electric ploughs can be produced, then the rural economy will not be able to buy them, as they are superfluous. Devaluation must have the consequence that the rural economy now only buys 1,000 ploughs, each with a value of £40=£4,000. Consideration of devaluation shows the unsaleability of the product, the disruption of all the proportions worked out so arduously by Otto Bauer.[170]

The communist response was more disappointing and difficult to deal with. Grossman did not respond publicly to Varga, who instead of providing a principled critique:

> preferred to abuse me in a Communist journal. He hasn't gone into my argumentation and objections with a single word. As soon as I have the time, I will write a critique of Varga and illuminate this puffed-up statistician from closer up.[171]

The illumination never came, probably because Grossman did not want to be ex-communicated. Some communists in the Soviet Union did make a point of defending the book. Miron Isaakovich Nakhimson, a former Bundist, had taken a senior position at the Department of Statistics of the International Agrarian Institute, in Moscow. Grossman had endorsed some of Nakhimson's positions – particularly on Varga's underconsumptionism – but remained critical of others.[172] Nakhimson invited Grossman to visit him in the Soviet Union. While there, Sergei Mitrofanovich Dubrovskii, the head of the Agrarian Institute, met Grossman and informed him: 'My dear comrade Grossman, no one here takes Varga seriously.'[173] The institute made Grossman a member in recognition of his books' contribution to Marxism.

During the 1930s and 1940s, Grossman wrote several essays and papers that included tacit replies to the accusations that his book promoted a mechanical theory of breakdown and revolution (see chapter four).

Chapter 3

The Life and Politics of Henryk Grossman, Part 2

I. The German Revolution and the rise of Naziism

For a full appreciation of Grossman's assessment of what went wrong in Germany, it is necessary to go over the events that preceded the success of the counter-revolution in closer detail, especially because the role of the split between the Social Democratic Party (SPD) and the Communist Party (KPD) has often been assessed too flippantly by both sides.

The 1918-19 Revolution

Sent to die in a pointless and unwinnable expedition, Germany's conscripted sailors launched a mutiny that ended the defeated nation's participation in WWI in 1918. The rest of the conscripted armed forces followed and powerful soldiers and workers' councils (Raeten) were established throughout the country. Karl Liebknecht of the communist Spartacus League stormed the Imperial Palace and proclaimed a 'free socialist republic of all Germans'.[174] Emperor Wilhelm II abdicated and fled the country. The chancellor, Prince Max, handed his position to the SPD chairman Friedrich Ebert in a bid to placate the masses. Made up of members of the SPD and the (more radical) Independent Social Democrats (USPD), the new government claimed to be 'purely socialist' and won the support of the vast majority of participants in the councils.[175] Liebknecht's warning that a counter-revolution was underway fell on deaf ears. Parliament was restored and half of its seats were taken by bourgeois parties.[176]

The government came to an agreement with the High Command of the Imperial Armed Forces, not only to 'fight against Bolshevism' but to take back power from the councils.[177] Many of their 'most reliable' troops, however, defected to the councils. Ebert and the High Command therefore had to create a mercenary paramilitary: the 'Freikorps' (also known as the Noske Guards, after SPD minister of defence Gustav Noske), drawn from the upper-class, pro-monarchist layers of the army.[178] As the situation sharpened, the most left-wing members of the government in the USPD resigned.[179]

At the end of 1918 the Spartacus League became the Communist Party of Germany (KPD). Luxemburg argued that a practical struggle for reforms alongside the workers had to be pursued to break their illusions in social democracy, including through participation in parliament. The majority of delegates disagreed.[180] They went with the slogan 'out of the unions' at a time when trade union membership was trebling.[181]

In January, Ebert planned to provoke premature action by sacking a popular left-wing police chief. Liebknecht took the bait. Without informing the KPD, he launched a move to oust the SDP and form a provisional government with a number of left Independents, a blatant act of opportunism and adventurism (attempting a coup and without winning the support of the masses).[182] When the KPD found out, however, they did little to hold things back. Nor could they, given their tiny numbers. Luxemburg raised an insurrectionary slogan under the auspices of 'raising consciousness'.

With a 52-man revolutionary committee endlessly conferring (the Bolsheviks had had an 11-man committee), the plan fell apart, leaving tens of thousands of ready-to-go soldiers out in the cold. The government took advantage of the confusion and sent in the Freikorps to slaughter the rebels – including Liebknecht and Luxemburg.[183] In the following weeks, the Freikorps were increasingly directed against any working-class organisation, not just the revolutionary minority. Thousands of workers were murdered.[184] On 19 January, Noske issued a decree destroying the power of the soldiers councils.[185]

The Kapp putsch

The SPD continued to justify authorities firing at striking workers by blaming the Independents and communists.[186] In June, the SPD vote fell from 11.5 million, just 5 months earlier, to 5.5 million. The SPD was then temporarily ousted by a right-wing putsch led by General Kapp, only to be defeated by an armed general strike that included most SPD workers. Although communists led this action in key parts of the country, the leadership shot its own party in the foot by declaring that the working class should 'not lift a finger' to defend the Republic or the SPD.[187]

After the failure of the Kapp putsch, the SPD once again sold out workers by failing to implement agreed concessions to purge the army and disarm far-right militias. The USPD and KPD grew quickly, and the left of the USPD then merged with the KPD. KPD membership had grown five-fold since the putsch to half a million.

Almost immediately, in March 1921, the KPD called for an armed general strike. Most workers, though, had just gone back to work, not something that could be changed at the flick of a switch. The KPD labelled anyone who did not support the action a 'scab' – which turned out to be the majority of the working class. Paul Levi complained that the unemployed 'were used as storm columns...against the bourgeoisie and four-fifths of the proletariat'.[188] Almost half the membership left.[189]

The theory of the offensive versus the united front

Bela Kun, leader of the defeated Hungarian Revolution – having taken power before securing enough support to hold onto it – went to Germany to demand that the KPD make a revolution in order to relieve the suffering of the isolated Russia. Supported by Grigory Zinoviev and Bukharin at the head of the Comintern, the 'theory of the offensive' determined that only revolutionary action by the vanguard could 'awaken' the masses. Lenin, who had been too busy to lead the Comintern, later denounced this as a 'lunatic ultraleft tactic', since the 'majority' of the working class had to be won over first through 'systematic' class struggle.[190]

As a corrective, Trotsky fleshed out the tactic of 'the united front from above'. Only by addressing the leaders of the reformist parties in calls for joint action could revolutionaries address the reformist rank and file. If the leaders accepted the invitation to united action, even around partial demands from the reformist programme, their rank and file would enter into battle alongside the communists, see that the lies their leaders had told about communists were false, and learn that it was the communists, not their own leaders, who would fight 'for every crust of bread'. If reformist leaders rejected the invitation, that too could only benefit the communists – the reformist leaders proving in practice that it was they who were splitting the class.[191]

1923

The KPD now took up this tactic and began to grow steadily, while also improving the organisation and militancy of the working class across its organisations. When hyperinflation took off in Germany in 1923 – inflicted by capitalists to decimate wages, taxes and debt[192] – working class militancy exploded. After a period of organising, the KPD called for a general strike and demanded a 'workers' government'. Lenin had supported a similar move in Russia, but without entering such a government, with the purpose of showing workers that even the most left-wing social democratic government could not solve the crisis in their favour. The SPD opposed both demands but a general strike took off, lasting 4 days. The now right-wing government fell and the SPD, with typical opportunism, joined a new coalition government. Unemployment then boomed. When the government banned workers' councils, the KPD advised the councils to defy the ban.[193]

Trotsky believed the Comintern had only a few weeks to prepare for insurrection. Stalin felt the situation would not ripen before spring. KPD Chairman Heinrich Brandler, chastened by previous adventurist failures, had to be won round by Trotsky.[194] Trotsky wanted to go to Germany, but the Comintern rejected this proposal. The Comintern did, however, 'move as never before in an effort to seize a revolutionary opportunity',[195] according to Chris Harman in *The Lost Revolution*. A Red Army general and a number of officers were sent to Germany.

By late September, inflation had gone even higher and production had plummeted. Hunger, anger and desperation continued to grow. A national coalition government responded by installing a military dictatorship and made plans to take the states of Saxony and Thuringia from their left SPD governments by force. The Comintern planned a counter-offensive.[196] Stalin wrote that victory in Germany would 'transfer the centre of world revolution from Moscow to Berlin'.[197]

Communists entered government with left social democrats in Saxony and Thuringia in order to gain access to weapons; a tactic favoured by Trotsky but not Brandler, who believed weapons had been removed from the state. Indeed, they found only 6000 guns instead of the expected 60,000.[198]

On 21 October, large contingents of troops began to march across the Saxon border. It was now or never. According to Harman: 'Hundreds of thousands of Communists were ready to move. And it seemed likely that their lead would be followed by the huge disoriented section of Social Democracy.'[199]

At a conference of various local workers' organisations from Saxony, Brandler called for a general strike – but the social democrats said such a decision could only be taken by the Socialist-Communist government.[200] Brandler now believed the social democrat rank and file would not support the uprising and called everything off.[201] Armed troops moved into Saxony unopposed and SPD ministers resigned from central government.

A huge credit squeeze stabilised the German mark, causing wholesale factory closures until 28% of union members were unemployed and 42% were on short-time. The 8-hour day, won in November 1918, was scrapped from the statute book.[202]

Brandler defended himself on the basis that the SPD still had a much higher membership than the KPD.[203] For a year or so, Stalin moved behind the left-wing faction of the KPD,[204] which had at first denounced the united front tactic outright and then put forward a compromised 'united front from below' position, which refused to address reformist leaders.

Arguments about whether conditions were really ripe enough for a successful insurrection have continued ever since. Grossman seems to have agreed with Trotsky's view that, once preparations had been made, there could be no turning back.[205]

Lenin had little input into international strategy after the start of 1923, dying shortly after in January 1924. Stalin took Lenin's place at the head of the CPSU instead of Trotsky, who had, at first, wanted to continue WWI on the basis of spreading revolution and opposing Germany's demand for Russia to grant independence to Finland, Estonia, Latvia, Lithuania, Poland, Belarus and Ukraine. Trotsky's theory of 'permanent revolution' contended that the failure to spread the revolution to Western Europe would make socialism in Russia short-lived – yet it lasted another 7 decades. The Bolsheviks had won a majority in the soviets because of their promise to pull Russia out of the war, making Trotsky's position untenable. Stalin was likely favoured among the newly converted Bolshevik masses for his more cautious outlook.[206]

The rise of the Nazis

Despite the botched revolution, the sheer size of the newly active labour movement meant the working class remained a force to be reckoned with. As the economic situation stabilised and unemployment began to fall, more social-welfare gains were actually made after the SPD had been ousted from government, although it retained a large parliamentary presence. Overall, between 1913 and 1929, Germany's national income grew by only 55%, yet wages increased by 130%, taxes by over 400%, and social-welfare expenditure by over 500%.[207]

Broadly speaking, the exporting, liberal class of capitalists effectively formed an alliance with the SPD and the General German Trade Union Federation (ADGB) for two reasons. Firstly, to quell revolutionary fervour. Secondly, to strengthen its own hand against the capitalists in agriculture and heavy industry, who relied more on the domestic market and therefore favoured protectionist policies (including a reduction or boycott of the huge war reparations owed to France, Belgium and Italy).

After the SPD returned to government in 1928, the industrial and rural elite began to close ranks. Then the Wall Street Crash struck. The Great Depression set in and by the end of the year millions of people in Germany were thrown back out of work. In 1931, the banks crashed and credit from foreign sources dried up. Capital could no longer afford or tolerate the gains in wages and social welfare. While the SPD began to accept austerity measures, their representatives opposed some concessions, especially with regards to unemployment insurance.[208]

Without a mass base, the traditional bourgeois parties were of little use to the industrialists. Eventually they turned, along with the High Command, to Hitler's NSDAP, which could attract 'a disparate collection of the urban [small] bourgeoisie, peasantry and some salaried [white collar] employees'. Despite concerns about the extent of its 'plebeian and populist demagoguery', which included talk of state intervention and 'anti-capitalism', the Nazis were seen as the only solution to a crisis that was explicitly viewed as one of profitability and accumulation.[209]

Even after Franz Papen (May-November 1932) and then Heinrich Brüning (May-July 1933) each became chancellor, forming semi-dictatorial regimes, the industrial-rural faction of the bourgeoisie opposed the faintest whiff of co-operation with labour or even the export faction. Wages were cut to 1927 levels, but that had been the year of labour's biggest post-1919 gains.[210] Wages remained the highest in Europe.[211] Parliament itself had become an obstacle to accumulation and, outside of the SPD, few were committed to saving it. With parliament at an impasse, even a considerable number of union leaders turned against the SPD.[212]

The industrialists and large farmers believed the NSDAP's worst tendencies could be tempered. Unable to keep Hitler under control, however, they were reduced to competing for state orders.[213] Nevertheless, they could appreciate his ruthless anti-socialism, colonial aspirations and economic programme of total privatisation.[214]

Letters to Mattick

Reflecting on the failures of the KPD in 1933, Grossman wrote in a letter to Paul Mattick, a German (anti-state, anti-party) council communist based in the US:

> The KPD masses were ready to fight but, unaccustomed to any spontaneous activity, they waited for the leaders' orders. The orders did not come. Many, many organisations, especially of youth, in their disappointment have gone over to Hitler...they speak of the 'betrayal' of the leaders... Every party makes mistakes...which can be corrected...But the fundamental mistake of the KPD was that at its head stood figures without responsibility, who were not capable of taking independent decisions at the decisive moments.

All the independent ones, who were capable of thinking for themselves, were thrown out of the party. What remained was a bureaucracy, which submitted slavishly to the Muscovites. But a revolution cannot be made on command from Moscow.[215]

The KPD were somewhat irrelevant after 1923. In December 1924 its share of the electoral vote was 9% compared to the SPD's 26%; then 10.6% versus 29.8% in May 1928. But with the SPD accepting austerity measures after 1929 and then – in the face of the growing Nazi vote[216] – the lesser evil of the Papen and Brüning regimes, the KPD's share climbed to 13.1% in 1930 and then 16.9% in November 1932, with the SPD's falling to 20.4%. Mattick opposed the KPD's participation in parliament, but Grossman disagreed:

There was a time when the workers' movement and social democracy wanted to use parliamentarism for *propaganda* purposes...Then they grew so deeply into parliamentary cretinism that they sought to achieve the resolution of social problems and the liberation of the working class only through 'democratic' parliamentary means. In the face of this fraudulent, parliamentary cretinism, 'anti-parliamentarism' was for the most part justified.

Today, however, when the proletarian movement only wants to engage in parliamentarism for agitational purposes, when it clearly knows that the bourgeoisie can only be defeated in the streets and the workplaces through forceful revolution, it would be irresponsible to refuse to make use of the parliamentary tribune...*The bourgeois, possessing classes today are* 'anti-parliamentary' and fascist; they want a dictatorship, whether open or hidden. And it is the task and the duty of the revolutionary workers' movement to brand this reversal in orientation, to show that the bourgeoisie was for 'democracy' so long as it had a large majority in the parliaments. Now that in Europe the working class has 40% and more of the seats and democracy could work *against* the bourgeoisie, the possessing classes...answer the demands of the workers with dictatorship and machine guns...

If you want to be consistently 'anti-parliamentary', you should not publish any *legal* newspapers...because, after all, freedom of the press is an aspect of bourgeois parliamentary democracy...But, in fact, you make use of legal freedom of the press, as long as it lasts – and rightly so...The difference between us...and the parliamentary fraudsters consists in the fact that we know it *will not last forever*. Eventually, the time will come when the ruling classes *abolish* freedom of the press and assembly. We are prepared for this and will respond with an *illegal* press and illegal meetings.[217]

In the second election of 1932, Nazi votes fell from 13.7 million to 11.7 million. Disillusioned Nazi stormtroopers were going over to the KPD by the thousand.[218] Between them, the SPD (8 million) and the KPD (5.2 million) had over 13 million votes.[219] Nazi backers moved into overdrive to secure the party's ascendency. In March 1933, it received 17 million votes, 43.9%. Even now the SPD leaders pledged to act as a 'loyal opposition' and the ADGB instructed its members to celebrate May Day alongside the Nazis as a 'national day of labour'.[220] Their compliance was ignored – the SPD was swiftly outlawed, smashed by the same High Command that it had collaborated with to defeat the KPD.

Votes were one thing. The KPD membership remained only half of its size in 1923.[221] The SPD and the unions were thoroughly integrated into the parliamentary system and could not bring themselves to challenge it, even now. In 1924, Stalin had labelled social democracy the 'moderate wing of fascism'.[222] Based on the SPD's murderous actions, this was hardly the 'insane' judgement Harman and others have called it. The preference of the SPD, after all, was to operate as legally as possible within a fascist system. This slogan, however, was tactically inept, and took attention away from the more useful parts of Stalin's analysis – that the ruling class used social democracy and fascism as carrot and stick to dampen revolutionary ambition and smash working-class organisation.

The 'social fascism' line, even if really aimed at the SPD leadership, was vulnerable to misinterpretation by both sides, encouraging sectarianism and risking alienating the bulk of reformist workers – the majority – from communists for good. It also seemed to contradict the Bolsheviks' own experience. They had remained a minority party in the soviets – with just 8000 members only 4 months before October – until the mass of war-weary workers, soldiers and peasants flooded into their ranks following an exodus from reformist parties, drawn primarily by the promise of peace (an offer the KPD never had the chance to make). The splits within and away from social democracy showed that it is not a monolithic ideology. There is no moderate wing of fascism – fascism is, by definition, the end of social democracy.

The very identity of the KPD, though, was bound up with its opposition to the SPD, Luxemburg having been expelled from the latter for opposing WWI before writing the former's manifesto. Those who followed her revolutionary legacy could not but see the SPD as war-mongering as well as reformist. The class divide between the generally skilled workers of the SPD and semi-skilled labourers and unemployed of the KPD was also clear.[223]

In new KPD leader Ernst Thälmann's 1932 speech 'The SPD and NSDAP are Twins', he said that KPD strategy 'directs the main blow against Social Democracy'. This would apparently create 'the very preconditions of an effective opposition to Hitler's fascism' since the SPD diluted the consciousness and unity of the working class as a whole.

While the strategy was emphatically misjudged, the KPD did direct this blow against the SPD leadership. The 'united front from below' tactic called for a 'systematic, patient and comradely persuasion of the Social Democratic, Christian and even National Socialist workers to forsake their traitorous leaders'.[224] Furthermore, during 1928-33, the KPD rank-and-file practised non-violent opposition towards the SPD, with political violence reserved for the NSDAP and its paramilitary stormtroopers (SA). In the austere years of the Depression, the Nazis and the KPD fought to win the hearts and minds of the unemployed and unskilled sections of the working class, who were the least politically active. This manifested in street fighting between the KPD and SA over control of their neighbourhoods. SPD rank and file would also fight the fascists here.[225]

The 'united front from below' strategy, though, seems to have attracted fewer than the 'social fascist' line repelled. Thälmann was incarcerated for attempting to organise a general strike in 1933 and executed 11 years later after a decade of torture in solitary confinement. In June 1932, Grossman told Mattick that the Nazis had a significant chance of taking power 'owing to the cleavage in the working class'.

> The victory of the Nazis would mean the destruction of the workers' movement for 10 to 15 years, and immensely increase the danger of a war against the Soviet Union! The German working class understands everything, knows everything, but it *does* almost nothing! Yet again we see that insight and perceptiveness alone are not sufficient – if the will to fight is not there.[226]

By March 1933, the 'major errors' of the KPD 'marionettes' 'installed by Moscow' had become obvious to Grossman.

> But: despite everything! The party, forced into illegality

by Hitler and compelled to engage in a fight for its life, will come out of this struggle purified and strengthened, and bring forth new, better leaders. The way things are in Germany, the KPD alone can be the point of crystallisation for a serious struggle for power and for the overthrow of fascism! Anything other than this is a criminal utopia![227]

In June, he sent Mattick an article by Trotsky[228] – now exiled by Stalin – his patience with the KPD and Comintern having deteriorated:

After the collapse of the KPD in Germany, the official leadership has learnt nothing...[The collapse] itself is denied and turned into a lie about a 'victory'. A call by the Central Committee of the KPD...says 'Our party has acquitted itself brilliantly.' In Moscow they make similar assessments of the situation. 'The policy of the KPD was right.' Only the lower level Party organs are at fault. The outrage in working class circles is great. And, nevertheless, we must take account of the fact that the great majority is not willing to break with the Third International. It is likewise a fact that the KPD cadres represent the main contingent in the resistance to the fascists.[229]

Grossman's assessment in November was yet more damning.

We see how the KPD – even leaving aside its tactics – did not...fulfil [the] most elementary duty [of educating workers] because its leadership, rather than work for clarity, knowledge and insight, just hurled abuse. All independent thought had become impossible because 'deviation' was immediately scented in it and the best, most self-sacrificing and battle-tested comrades were marked as lackeys of the bourgeoisie. If the bourgeois revolution in France sent its own fighters to the guillotine, killed them physically, the proletarian fighters, who think for themselves and seek the right path, are currently put to death in a moral sense.[230]

Despite this, Grossman cautioned against Mattick's talk of betrayal:

> The word 'betrayal' has often been misused and applied simply when the situation did not develop in the expected direction. But it explains very little. The 'betrayal' itself is, for me, a symptom of the immaturity of the workers' movement, an indication that the working class's objective situation makes a betrayal profitable, a sign that the traitors (leaving aside all the weaknesses of their character) have not yet seen the objective possibility of a proletarian victory. As such a possibility draws closer, the 'traitors' will become scarcer and scarcer.[231]

While this is easier said than done in the emotional heat of a losing battle, this is something that revolutionaries have to be very conscious of. In January Grossman expanded further on these thoughtful comments:

> I certainly agree with you that these people must be labelled traitors *in the day-to-day struggle*...But from the point of view of *comprehending* the events, what is explained by giving them such a name? Nothing! *Why do these people betray?* That is the problem.
>
> To the KPD, for example, the whole of social democracy was nothing but 'betrayal'. Instead of asking why the masses in their millions followed social democracy, the Party reassured itself by branding them as 'traitors'.
>
> And the same thing is true not only of the KPD and the SPD but generally; of the US as well...Is that accidental? I

do not think so. One should and must analyse why the most progressive elements of the workers' movement do not know how to overcome their character as sects so as to become a movement of the masses. That is the most important task of the moment...First Spartacus, then the KAPD [Communist Workers' Party of Germany] etc. up to the KPD – all of them were small groups without any influence as long as they remained revolutionary. The KPD became a million strong party when it accustomed itself to parliamentary cretinism on the model of the SPD, and acted the same way as the SPD, only employing a few more radical words in their dictionary.

At my place for some time, there have been weekly meetings of workers and former members of the KPD etc... and we discuss these *same* problems, in order to learn and to understand why in 1918-19, 1920, 1923 etc. all the objectively given revolutionary opportunities were squandered! Why the revolutionary elements always remained isolated.'[232]

This topic continued to occupy Grossman's thoughts the following February:

Every revolutionary movement must begin as a tiny minority...But why didn't this minority, despite the favourable objective conditions, succeed in...winning the masses in their millions. That is the central problem: what use is it if various carping critics constantly watch over the 'purity' of the revolutionary programme, like old school-mistresses over their virtue. The point is rather to set the masses in motion. A step of real revolutionary practice is more important than half a dozen virtuous theoretical programmes.[233]

Grossman did not forget his disdain for the reformists. For him, the rejection of his economics and Lenin's politics within the mainstream left had had profound consequences.

What was the year 1929 in the US and the year 1931 in Germany and England if not a giant breakdown? The working class was not prepared for this. It did not have a Lenin, who awaited and worked towards such a moment. Rather, for decades it heard from Hilferding and Helene Bauer that a breakdown was impossible. Only such a disorientation of the working class made it possible for the ruling class to overcome the panic and to survive the breakdown.[234]

Hitler became chancellor at the end of January 1933. The liberal export faction, with foreign trade having slumped by more than half, now had no need for its alliance with labour – saying it would judge the new government on its economic policies. The SPD was the only party to vote against The Enabling Act that permitted the Nazi government to issue laws without the consent of parliament. The KPD had already been outlawed.

In April, Jews were prohibited from public employment and honorary posts, including at universities. The Prussian Ministry for Science, Art and Education formally withdrew Grossman's licence to teach on 18 December, despite an exemption for Jews who had fought in the armed forces of an ally of the German Reich in WWI.[235] Regardless, another law in July sacked all civil servants who belonged to any Marxist organisation. Having prepared for such an eventuality, the IfS fled to Geneva and then New York. Grossman went to Paris, since he had friends there and his French was much better than his English.

The Popular Front and the economic roots of fascism

When the Comintern quietly abandoned the 'social fascism' line, it staggered from a hard left sectarianism into soft right opportunism in its uncritical support for a Popular Front, a coalition led by reformists (who were, like Varga, underconsumption theorists). The Comintern now directed its parties to seek an alliance not only with social democratic but also liberal and even traditional conservative parties. 'Now... an even more wretched policy follows,' Grossman said. 'The Communist movement is subordinated to the Soviet Union's foreign policy and need for peace. The result: unprincipled opportunism in current policies in all countries.'[236]

In 1935, he told Max Beer that the Third International was 'morally bankrupt', although he remained 'an *optimist* because the *objective* economic situation of capitalism is hopeless', suggesting that he did think capitalism was in its death throes. According to Kuhn, Grossman's attitude towards the Comintern's support for the Popular Front in Spain softened under the influence of a friendship with a Spanish comrade.[237]

The Comintern's flip-flopping could be perhaps partially explained by its eclectic economics. According to its 1928 Programme:

> The predominance of private property in the means of production and the anarchy prevailing in the process of production have disturbed the equilibrium between the various branches of production; for a growing contradiction developed between the tendency towards unlimited expansion of production and the restricted consumption of the masses of the proletariat (general overproduction), and this resulted in periodical devastating crises and mass unemployment.[238]

Drawing on both disproportionality and underconsumption theory, it is not surprising that confused tactics followed. That self-preservation through defence, not offence, became the order of the day, however, surely has to be recognised as mostly a manifestation of isolation. The Soviet Union could hardly turn the world socialist by itself. Defence would not stop the German invasion several years later, though. It took at least 20 million soviet lives, vastly more than the American or British sacrifice, to finally crush the Nazis.

When Popular Front governments took office, class struggle took off. Through the largest wave of industrial action in French history, workers won large wage rises, shorter working hours, and, for the first time anywhere, paid annual leave.

According to the theory of France's Popular Front leader Leon Blum, the higher consumption of the working class should have resolved the capitalist crisis. Alas, the crisis deepened. Reaction, fascism and war rampaged across Europe. With France becoming increasingly oppressive, Grossman moved to England in 1936, where he wrote four pages on the economic basis of fascism and the ineffectiveness of the Popular Front:

> *How is a crisis overcome?* Not...through a sudden increase in the *purchasing power of consumers*, following which a boom sets in. In reality we see something entirely different: hundreds of attempts, of a partial or general nature, are made to restore *profitability*...[by] reducing capital costs of machines, raw materials, *pushing down interest*, reducing taxes, reducing social services – and most importantly *pushing down wages!*
>
> The other way is to increase prices by extending credit, destroying part of the product or restricting part of production...
>
> *Both* paths are often taken at the same time. The *slowness* of the recovery confirms my theory that the duration of the crisis cannot be predicted and calculated, let alone the duration of the boom!...It depends on how quickly or slowly entrepreneurs identify where to make improvements, on the response of the government (reductions in interest and tax), on the strength or resistance of workers' organisations in relation to wage reductions, on the strength of cartels in relation to reductions in the prices of machines and

raw materials, etc... If [workers] are tough in defending themselves, they slow the implementation of wage cuts – and thus the restoration of *profitability.*

...Precisely in these developed countries with strong workers organisations fascism comes to the aid of capitalism.

...That is the role of German fascism. Wages, which were 44 billion Marks in 1928, fell (with roughly the same number of people employed) to 31 billion in 1935, i.e. by 13 billion or 30%. When the increases in the prices of food, clothing etc. are taken into account, real wages fell even more, about 35-40%. And exactly for this reason profitability grew...

Those who want increases in the purchasing power of workers do not operate in the real world and its causal relations, but in that of utopian 'demands' which totally block the path to understanding fascism and its entire policy for saving capitalism.

The capitalist crisis is to be overcome, on the basis of capitalism, by demanding non-capitalist methods of distribution! One teaches the capitalists that, by forcing down wages they mistake their own interests. One advises them to *increase* wages – in their own interests!

But the 'stupid' capitalists do not pay much attention to this advice...They seek to overcome the crisis through wage cuts...[239]

Reflationary efforts in the US, Britain and Germany, Grossman later pointed out to Horkheimer, did not start by raising purchasing power, but on the contrary by openly or covertly reducing the level of wages. According to Blum, the increases in wages and reductions in working hours should have reinflated the economy. In fact these policies

led to a general rise in prices and the inability of French industry to compete. Briefly, the failure of stimulation. He had to openly withdraw the wage increases. Since this was impossible, he stumbled into devaluation, i.e. an escape route which in a disguised form meant wage reduction...

Promising to publish something more substantial, Grossman added: 'I believe that an embarrassing funeral for underconsumptionist theory is important!'[240] In March 1937, Blum announced a pause in his entire reform programme. His government resigned before the end of June. All this had demonstrated that

> theory is, after all, not unworldly brooding, it should draw from experience! This experiment shows that... underconsumptionist doctrine, suffers from a scandalous bankruptcy.[241]

In response to Mattick, Grossman also addressed the importance of attacking bourgeois mythology in the fight against fascism.

> The [council communist] 'Ko' [Karl Korsch] makes me out to be a supporter of Luxemburg's theory and arrives at the conclusion that crisis theories are completely superfluous as instruments for achieving knowledge. So he ends up praising [Georges] Sorel's theory of myths... How far one can get with myth alone...Hitler has precisely shown us. The whole petit bourgeois demagogy, which works with promises that it cannot keep, is the practical application of the theory of myth. The bourgeois will always be superior masters in this field. If the petit bourgeois layers had knowledge of tendencies of development, they would not have lined up with Hitler. He must deceive them and will deceive them. Disillusionment will be the result. We, however, do not want to deceive others or ourselves. Accordingly, our actions must be based on theoretical

knowledge of the tendencies of development, i.e. how things work out objectively.[242]

Critical support for the Soviet Union

At the start of the Soviet Union's Popular Front strategy in 1934, Grossman's despair was tempered by optimism: 'I think that the working class will awake. A new world war rapidly approaches. It will end with a series of revolutionary uprisings.'[243] This prediction turned out to be right, but only a limited number succeeded. At the end of WWII, the Soviet Union expanded into the rest of eastern Europe – taking advantage of major capital flight – including East Germany; while the Maoist revolution in China finally succeeded after more than 20 years of anti-colonial and civil war in 1949.

There can be little doubt that Grossman should have been invited to work in a leading role in the Comintern. Despite its snubs, Grossman retained a principled position of critical support for the Soviet Union. In March 1933, he said he had spoken in a Frankfurt meeting attended by 2000 people 'in favour of Soviet Russia (despite everything!)...The whole of the reactionary press up to and including the social democratic *Volksstimme* came down upon me in a most vulgar manner.'[244]

In February 1935, Grossman explained why he considered the Soviet Union to be socialist, as opposed to Mattick's claim that it was capitalist. On his visit there Grossman 'did not limit myself to the proclamations of theorists' but 'asked the practical planners how the plan is "made"'.

I gained the impression that over there they make calculations in use-values, insofar as it was a matter of the duration of production (annual or five yearly). That these volumes of use-values are expressed in money...changes nothing.[245] Because money here only plays the role of an index for the purpose of exact comparisons, since you cannot compare 10 tonnes of potatoes + 2 wagons of coal in 1934 with 8 tonnes of potatoes + 1 wagon of wheat + 1 wagon of coal in 1928, if all the quantities are not reduced to value indices. But money has changed its function in the sphere of production as well as in the sphere of circulation. If things happen in Russian planning nowadays which have nothing to do with a socialist economy, still the basis of the five-year plan was right at the time and I am convinced that every other economic plan in coming communist economies, whether in Germany or in England, will be unable to take a path that is different in principle, making allowance for the historical fact that these countries will be able to begin a planned economy on a higher level.[246]

This assessment alludes to Marx's position that socialism would be 'economically, morally, and intellectually, still stamped with the birthmarks of the old society from whose womb it emerges'.[247] Grossman expanded on his defence of the Soviet Union in October, going so far as to call Mattick sectarian:

The Soviets are not, like capitalist countries, a surplus value producing state entity. I too dislike the Stalinist bureaucracy...there is much, very much, to criticise. But in principle I consider that there are no private property-owners nor private accumulation, and, furthermore, many of the deformations were unavoidable, given the constraint of the threat from the external enemy.

I am convinced that your point of view towards the Soviet Union is un-Marxist. You reject the SU because it does not correspond with your abstract, theoretical idea of a socialist entity. This is the standpoint of a sectarian. In such cases, the danger is that the sectarian is 'right' in abstract terms, but he remains a sectarian with few supporters – and will always remain apart from the great mass movement. I am convinced that if you yourself were able to exert decisive influence on developments in Russia, you would not, under the pressure of objective conditions, in the economic sphere...pursue a different economic policy...

Your opinion that the capitalist states do not fear Russia today is fundamentally wrong. Sooner or later the Western Europeans will enter into a coalition against the Soviet Union, which Japan will also join in from the East.

I believe that in the US you are too far away from things. Here in Europe everyone knows that a defeat of the Soviet Union would throw the workers' movement back 50 years. So one cannot fight against the Soviet Union as a state that produces 'surplus value'; we have rather to defend it from its external enemy.[248]

The economic and political basis of Grossman's nuanced defence of the Soviet Union has not been convincingly argued against in the literature on him to date. Moreover, it is unfair to characterise him as a 'Stalinist',[249] a term that really has no agreed upon meaning and clouds many complex historical lessons. Grossman did need, of course, to keep his public criticism respectable if he was to reach and influence the world's biggest socialist audience. At one time, however, he complained to Horkheimer that, 'Over there, Stalin has to be praised as the greatest philosopher, the greatest economist, the greatest thinker ever.' Ilse Hamm's claim that Grossman had an 'undying love of Stalin' was clearly a gross exaggeration – although she perhaps made it flippantly in response to Grossman's remark that she should not marry Mattick, 'because he is a sectarian'.[250] (The three remained friends!)

II. Trials and tribulations with the IfS

In 1930, Horkheimer replaced an unwell Grünberg as director of the IfS. Grossman took over Grünberg's contributions to *Elster's*

Dictionary, a standard reference work on economic institutions and concepts. He wrote 13 biographical entries and substantial essays on anarchism, Bolshevism, and the Second and Third Internationals. His review of Marxism since Marx's death promoted his breakdown theory as a major breakthrough (see chapter 3). He also updated and revised some of Grünberg's entries. Grossman kept to his deal with the authorities not to write about Poland. His summaries concerning German and Austrian social democracy, though, made Grünberg's previously dispassionate accounts somewhat more partisan. Otto Bauer, for example, was full of 'verbal radicalism and opportunist practice'. Grossman was more generous about the likes of Eugene Debs (US), Jean Jaures and Georges Sorel (France), social democrats he felt had more genuine class principles and engaged in class struggle to uphold them.[251]

In his longest biography, Grossman praised Lenin for his contributions on political organisation, the role of soviets, and revolutionary tactics. His account of the history of the Bolshevik Party hardly mentioned Stalin, and – unlike the new communist leadership – did not pretend that Trotsky had played no role in the Russian Revolution.[252]

Grossman's essay on the Third International called the programme adopted at its Sixth Congress in 1928, 'one of the most significant documents in the history of the modern workers' movement, summarising the whole knowledge and experience of the proletariat's revolutionary struggles'. This was undoubtedly true, but Grossman's entry took more interest in the challenges of building socialism in an agrarian country than in the correctness of any foreign policy. A positive entry about communism in a mainstream reference work was unheard of. Grossman later recalled that KPD leaders were grateful 'for my essay "Bolshevism" as I had so effectively supported the cause in such a place'.[253]

The end of slavery and the bourgeois worldview

Grossman's output at the IfS included a review of a collection of articles by Marx and Engels on the US Civil War (1861-65). Marx and Engels wrote in support of the 'bourgeois republic' in the North against the slave oligarchy of the South, convinced that the complete abolition of slavery was a precondition for the emancipation of the US working class and that 'labour in white skin cannot achieve dignity as long as it is despised in a black skin' (Marx). Moreover, says Grossman, slavery's 'inherent expansionist tendencies limited the possibilities for northern industrial capital and hence the development of the industrial proletariat'. Slavery was inherently dependent on geographical expansion since land was cultivated by means of *extensive farming* – the intensive nature of slave labour exhausted the land. To preserve themselves, slavers had to export slavery by seizing new territory. For Marx, the US form of slavery differed to the purely consumptionist system of antiquity (the ancient past) because it was part of the present profit-making system that served the world market.

Abraham Lincoln's election in 1860 came with the demand from Republicans to limit slavery to the South, to push it back out of the 'free states'. The union therefore became worthless to the South. Its war against the North was not a defensive one for the status quo but a war of aggression and conquest. 'It was not difficult to predict that, in this case, the living standards of the white working class of the North would gradually be forced down to the level of the slaves,' says Grossman.

Lincoln eventually realised that, to save the Union – and its most agriculturally fertile regions – slavery would have to be abolished. 'It was an unavoidable struggle between two social systems that could no longer peacefully coexist, because the continued existence of the one was only possible by virtue of its victory over the other!'[254]

Grossman also wrote about the end of slavery in the context

of capitalism's development in general. Franz Borkenau (an ex-communist turned social democrat) followed Max Weber in arguing that capitalism – and thus wage labour – had emerged as a result of the Protestant work ethic, which educated the masses in labour discipline via the new printing press, the first generalised example of machine-aided mass production. Modern mechanics and the division of labour in manufacturing (divided between competing independent producers) dated only from the first half of the seventeenth century, he claimed.

Grossman's extensive research, however, showed that mechanics had in fact been developed at the beginning of the sixteenth century, and manufacturing in the second half of the eighteenth century.[255] Examples of capitalist production stretched as far back as the thirteenth century in Italy, a country 'Borkenau himself calls...the land "of religious indifference"'.[256] 'For the beginnings of bourgeois thought, precisely the 13th and 14th centuries are important.'[257]

With artisanship and manufacture (labour without electrified machinery) becoming more important than agriculture in the production of social wealth, Grossman argued that slavery had not been enforceable in the more complex arenas of towns and cities, making paying labour in cash necessary. Whereas technological progress had been marginal as long as production could depend on one social *perpetuum mobile* (form of perpetual motion), namely slavery, capitalist production needed an artificial *perpetuum mobile*.[258] As Marx pointed out, the skilled hand of the labourer is reduced to the function of a motive force; a function which may be performed by any power, not necessarily man.[259] Capitalism therefore stimulated technological and mechanical development. Borkenau's focus on the printing press as the harbinger of new attitudes to work had it the other way round.

Weber, Borkenau said, had proved that the religious work

ethic had to be preached since this 'could not be "achieved by means of a legal compulsion to labour in the form of serfdom"'. This claim totally ignored the fact that peasants, in a process of proletarianisation, were brutally driven from their land.[260] Labour discipline was not the morality of the mass of workers but preached by the 'religion of the threatened middle stratum' of craftsmen as a 'doctrine of self-justification' for accepting the ideology of capitalists. Furthermore,

> it was not even the specific doctrines of Calvinism which made it suitable for 'keeping the masses obedient' but rather the *generally irrational presuppositions,* which it shared with Lutheranism, of predestined salvation through faith...
>
> ...This irrationalism was given the *appearance of rationality* because it presupposed a rational relationship between this-worldly good works and their other-worldly reward – salvation...In this education of the masses in obedience, in diverting them from this world, from the improvement of their earthly fate and from the fight against the corrupt might of rulers, the role of religion in bolstering capitalism is given clearer expression than in its direct political-economic manifestations in questions of usury, interest, trade and wages. This is the visible spirit of capitalism, not only of the Protestant Ethic but of every religion aimed at the domestication of the masses.[261]

Influenced by Marx's methodology, Grossman also pointed out that theoretical mechanics had been established through practical mechanics and the study of technology, not the other way round.[262] Abstracting from the complicated appearance of machines, by conceptually separating their parts – and motive force, which could not be studied and measured without being objectified in the form of machinery – could only be done as they became more elemental (made of fewer parts).

The development of mechanics led to the mechanistic worldview: natural phenomena were ever more conceived as machine-like rather than in the form of organisms. Explaining a natural phenomenon now meant describing the mechanism producing it; and the operations of mechanisms were understood to follow rigid natural laws, rather than to integrate into and transform their natural environment.[263]

One of three essays taking aim at Borkenau's work, 'The Social Foundations of Mechanical Philosophy and Manufacture' remains a reference point for historians of science.

IfS sacking

Although the IfS had never been Marxist in deed, it became increasingly less so in word, especially as an atmosphere of anti-communism took hold in the US. Grossman rated some of Horkheimer's philosophical work,[264] but told him after reading his 1937 essay 'The Latest Attack on Metaphysics', that,

> from an activist standpoint, you should be interested in confronting broad layers of young people. One should never forget that the victory of Cartesianism was not simply achieved through the power of pure thought but was supported in the university by the fists and clubs of Dutch students, who answered the brutal force of scholasticism with the similar force of their fists![265]

Not wishing to make his Marxism explicit by the time of his promotion to the top of the IfS, Horkheimer wrote guardedly about the origins of 'the dialectical theory of society' and the 'will for a more human existence' in which 'a higher spontaneity' is possible. Citing Marx's account of historical materialism in the preface and postscript to *Capital*, Grossman was clear that the laws of capitalist development determine human behaviour more than vice-versa. But, insisted Grossman, that '[does] not contradict activism' and 'should be dealt with in an essay like yours'.[266]

Horkheimer did not respond and his views became increasingly conservative. He and Theodore Adorno began to reject the working class as an emancipatory force along with the constructive (socialism-building) side of Marx's analysis.[267] Relations worsened when Horkheimer openly denounced the Soviet Union over the Molotov-Ribbentrop Pact, a non-aggression pact between Nazi Germany and the Soviet Union that partitioned Poland. Grossman saw the pact – which lasted only 2 years of an agreed 10 – as necessary and defensive, buying the Soviet Union time to prepare for the Nazi invasion. What is often wilfully ignored is that Stalin had previously approached the US, Britain and France with an anti-Nazi pact that they turned down.

After the 1938 downturn in the US, the IfS's finances worsened. Horkheimer and Pollock wanted Grossman off the payroll, but Grossman refused to resign. After repeated delays to the publication of Grossman's 80-page study on *Marx, Classical Political Economy and the Problem of Dynamics* (see chapter 3), he threatened to publish the work elsewhere with a preface accusing the institute of 2 years of sabotage.[268]

When Horkheimer told him in April 1943 about an institute project on antisemitism funded by the conservative American Jewish Committee, Grossman replied that he did not know 'if you are interested in the Jewish Project only in so far as several thousand dollars can be earned through it'.[269]

Horkheimer later called Grossman's 'The Evolutionist Revolt against Classical Economics' (see chapter four) a 'most rotten piece of work'.[270] In March 1944, Horkheimer sacked Grossman, who had allegedly described the institute in private as 'those swine at 429', 'the seat of capitalistic reaction', and 'those slanderers of the Soviet Union'.[271]

III. East Germany

Grossman's friend Christina Stead – an Australian novelist who based a character on Grossman in *Letty Fox* – wrote to her husband, Bill Blake, a Jewish American economist, about Grossman's disdain for the institute. She said he had become 'a poor lost man' who 'needs a wife like nothing else'. The couple were very fond of Grossman. Like him, they supported the Soviet Union and were members of the Joint Anti-Fascist Refugee Committee. Blake would later refer to Grossman as his brother and Stead would describe him as 'one of the men who meant something to me'.[272] The feeling was mutual. In a letter to Bill, Grossman wrote in his broken English: 'Sometime seems to me superfluous to express how much I love you and Christina. You must have the feelings; the words are unable to express the real things.'[273]

Stead described Grossman as 'a marvellous companion' so long as he was 'not in one of his black or silly moods'. 'He's crazy as a bedbug is our Grossman, wild, excitable...but sane, cheerful, brave...a splendid fellow, though quite a trial as a conversationalist. He does not give a tuppenny damn for me and my affairs: nothing in the world counts but his work.' She believed he would 'work himself to death'.[274] Indeed, Grossman suffered a stroke during his time in New York.

His loneliness doubled after Christina and Bill returned to Europe in 1947. He also learned that Janina and their son Jan, who worked with the anti-fascist Resistance in Warsaw, had been murdered in Auschwitz in 1943; Henryk's brother and sister-in-law in another death camp. His other son, Stanislaw, had likely died earlier.[275]

He no longer had any family in Poland and did not want to return there. He applied to the German Central Administration for Education in the Soviet Zone for a professorship in Berlin or Leipzig. 'I want to make my small contribution to the construction of a new better Germany...I would regard it as my particular mission to win hundreds, yes, thousands of the youth of a large city for the idea of Marxism and for the ideals that we fight for in practice.'[276] He ended up in the Social Science Faculty in Leipzig, despite its new dean regarding Grossman's theory as mechanical.[277]

In Germany, Grossman and his work received some belated recognition. The faculty suggested that Grossman be nominated for the National Prize for Science and Technology, while many students regarded his inaugural address, along with those of other returning scholars, as an important public event.[278]

Despite now suffering from Parkinson's disease, Grossman relished his new opportunities in a socialist country. He might complain that, 'there are always new rallies, meetings, functions, and visits by journalists etc. which rob me of time,' but he did appreciate their importance.[279] Among a number of organisations he joined, he became a member of the Socialist Unity Party (SEPD) – a 'working alliance' between the KPD and SPD in the East.

When the official Soviet line in economics shifted and Varga fell out of favour, Grossman took seriously an opportunity to address the 'Varga discussion'. Another variation of underconsumption theory was taken up, however.[280]

Grossman's condition deteriorated in 1949. He suffered another stroke and had to have an operation for a growth on his prostate. After one visit, Blake noted that, 'Despite his illness, the clarity of his mind is simply astonishing: it was beautiful to hear his low voice following a train of reasoning and humanity.'[281] In Saxony, at least, according to Blake, 'the Party regards him as its great man in theory (they speak of him plainly as the first Marxian of Germany) and in the corridors heads of the State here, ministers, etc. glide in and out for news of his recovery'.

In March 1950, the City of Leipzig nominated Grossman for the National Prize 'for the totality of his scientific achievements in the area of scientific socialism. One of his principal works,

The Law of Accumulation and Breakdown of the Capitalist System, received the greatest attention around the world.' Grossman did not win the prize, however, presumably because it had to be approved by Berlin. The German Democratic Republic never officially acknowledged Grossman's contribution to Marxism and published none of his work. Instead, textbooks there rejected his crisis theory.[282]

After surgery, Grossman's health improved for a time; but he had only been given a year to live. His death was announced by the university:

> Professor Dr jur. Henryk Großmann, Professor with the Chair of Political Economy and Director of the Institute for Political Economy, died on 24 November 1950 after long and severe suffering. With Prof Dr Großmann the University of Leipzig loses a scholar with a worldwide reputation who also remained true to his scientific calling during the period of fascist dictatorship in Germany.[283]

Chapter 4

Marxism and the Myth of a Stable Capitalism

During Grossman's time working for the IfS, he deepened his critique of capitalism as a mode of production by re-engaging with Marx's historical materialism and sociological thought. This work reinforced Grossman's conclusion that Marx was right to see capitalism as incapable of linear progress – and that social crises and ruptures, rather than mere gradual and incremental developments, are the hallmarks of historical change.

In this chapter we look at some of Grossman's most important contributions from this period. We start, however, with a book review Grossman wrote in 1926, which addresses some of the most common pessimisms of Marx's 'Marxist' critics.

I. New Theory of Imperialism and the Social Revolution (1926)[284]

Grossman had given more than a hint of what to expect in *The Law of Accumulation* in a long, withering review of Fritz Sternberg's 1926 book *Imperialism*, a work which claimed to have fixed Marx's blind spots. These included: the weakening of crises under capitalism due to socialisation, as asserted by Bernstein; the improvement in the condition of the working class despite Marx's apparent insistence that it always remained impoverished; growing numbers of capitalists; and increases in the numbers of petty-bourgeois and peasant enterprises. Marx had, therefore, apparently underestimated the size of the counter-revolution. The evidence Sternberg lines up to defend this reading of Marx, as Grossman mockingly notes, is none other than 'Marx's reproduction schema!'

The author humbly asserts that his book is 'a continuation of Marx's *Capital*'. Soon, however, he changes his mind. He does not want to merely perfect; he feels impelled by the historical situation, rather, to become a pioneer. For nothing remains of Marx's system that deserves to be carried forward.

Sternberg had committed the same infantile error as everyone else: acting as if Marx treated his simplifying assumptions as empirical reality. It is left, therefore, to Sternberg (like the others!) to discover the intermediary classes between capitalists and workers that Marx left out or failed to anticipate in terms of their development. Grossman points out that Marx had already done both. As he went on to do in more detail in his book, Grossman explained Marx's 'most diligent' method of successive approximation.

Sternberg similarly accuses Marx of creating an 'agricultural pyramid' comprising only rural proletarians and large landowners. This 'caricature', though, is Sternberg's invention and does not tally with Marx's theory. In Marx's system agriculture is treated as having been industrialised by capital, but *only at first*. In contrast, Sternberg repeats the Malthusian-Ricardian fallacy about diminishing returns of the soil, '[a]s if it was not labour but the soil that produces' exchange-value.

> One of Marx's finest and, to this day, unmatched accomplishments was to demonstrate that the supposedly 'natural' barriers to production which bourgeois economics invokes to explain the rising prices of agricultural products and the increase in ground rent (population growth and the declining fertility of the land), do not arise from 'nature' but from [capitalist] social institutions.

Marx's analysis includes the recognition that the land is a productive tool in itself, whereas the factory is a foundation.

Grossman explains:

> Every progress in industry reduces the price of production and hence increases the rate of ground rent, allowing landowners to 'put away in their own private purses the result of a social development achieved without their participation'. In agriculture, however, every development of the productive forces, by bringing down the value of agricultural products, works in the opposite direction. This means that the ground rent declines. These capitalist determinants of profitability evidently form 'one of the greatest obstacles to a rational agriculture' – but this has nothing to do with diminishing returns of the soil. [William] Petty already told us (1699) 'that the landlords of his time feared improvements in agriculture because they would cause the price of agricultural products and hinc (the level of) rent to fall'.

The contradictions between the two branches of production, however, increasingly disappear as farming is industrialised and commercialised. Eventually 'productivity in agriculture must increase relatively more rapidly than in industry'.

'Sternberg's absolutely Malthusian conception is revealed as the deepest source of all his errors' because he thinks the law of rising returns only applies in industry. 'The ultimate reason for all capitalist and imperialist expansion, according to Sternberg's diagnosis, lies in the natural difference between industrial and agricultural labour.' According to his jumbled theory, capital exports are compelled by rising wages in industry, which lead to falling profits. Rising wages make imperialist wars inevitable!

Sternberg accuses Marx of supposing that the realisation of socialism comes only with the absolute disappearance of the small capitalists. New tactics capable of attracting this stratum to socialism therefore had to be written. But, Grossman points out, Marx had already done this:

Since the *Communist Manifesto*, since the famous Address of the Central Authority to the League of March 1850... Marx described the problems of proletarian tactics, the role and tasks of the proletariat in the coming revolutions, its relationship to the middle strata, and ultimately also the character of the proletarian revolution itself. The peasantry and the urban petty bourgeoisie are referred to...as 'most important [classes]...in all modern revolutions'. Finally it is demonstrated how and under what circumstances 'peasants, petty bourgeois, the middle strata in general, stand with the proletariat', dissociate themselves from the ruling classes, are gradually driven to '[r]evolt against bourgeois dictatorship, to change society', and ultimately to 'group round the proletariat as the decisive revolutionary power'.

Sternberg's vital intervention on tactics does not address the monumental problems that confront revolutionaries. Instead he talks only of the question of timing. Apparently Marx had, like Bernstein, anticipated revolution only when the concentration of capital made the prospect of socialisation most ripe. But because the inevitability of imperialist war 'winds back' the ripeness for socialisation, Marx had not recognised that revolution can come 'too late'. At the same time, says Sternberg, the trend towards socialisation has improved the condition of the working class and therefore clouded its revolutionary consciousness. A revolution is not necessary economically but only to prevent imperialist war and the historical oblivion of man. Grossman counters:

That war entails destruction is not to be denied. But Sternberg's claim that this destruction winds back ripeness for socialisation contradicts experience as well as the inner nature of capitalism. Either the destruction is so great that it embraces the basis of the productive apparatus itself, the entire capitalist mechanism disintegrates and the barricades go up between the classes. In the other case, society is impoverished by the ravages of war but this is the impetus for the forced development of the productive forces, for the enormous concentration and rationalisation movements of the kind we now witness in Germany. For this is the only possible way to withstand the competitive struggle with other, richer capital powers, on a capitalist basis. Actually, despite the ravages of the World War, the tendencies to concentration and combination that were already present everywhere have accelerated and intensified. Lenin already noted this in 1915. Within only a few years, the prewar stage of development was recovered and surpassed. The fall into historical oblivion is a naive and empty phrase. If, however, one assumes with Sternberg the possibility that humanity could be cast into historical oblivion by the next imperialist war, there is no other way to save it than to *pre-empt* the next war through revolution.

Nowhere does Sternberg anticipate economic breakdown. Consciousness has to be created detached from economic conditions and the class struggle. Socialism is achieved on a purely subjective-voluntarist basis.

By way of contrast, let us quote the voice of an expert in revolutionary matters... Marxists, says Lenin in 1915, 'know perfectly well that a revolution *cannot* be "made", that revolutions *develop* out of objectively (i.e. independently of the will of parties and classes) mature crises and turns in history...'.[285] '[A] revolution is *impossible without a revolutionary situation*...For a revolution to take place, it is usually insufficient for 'the lower classes not to want' to live in the old way; it is also necessary that "the upper classes should be unable" to live in the old way', that an *objective impossibility* for the ruling classes to assert their rule in unchanged form develops. Secondly, that 'the suffering and want of the oppressed classes have grown more acute than usual'. 'Without these *objective changes*...a revolution, as a general rule, is impossible. The totality of all these objective changes is called a revolutionary situation.' It is not merely revolutionary consciousness (which, incidentally, cannot be produced outside a revolutionary situation, merely by hammering the final goal into heads) that only figures in addition as a further condition with a subjective character. It is rather something entirely different: '*the ability of the revolutionary class to take revolutionary mass action [strong enough]*',[286] which presupposes an *organisation* of the coherent will of the masses and *extensive experience in the class struggles* of everyday life.

Sternberg is 'impressed by the Russian Revolution, but without understanding its necessary mechanisms, he eventually seeks to accelerate the revolution by stressing voluntarism'.

The review serves as a clear endorsement of Lenin's analysis, further contradicting the idea that Grossman under-appreciated the role of class struggle. Again, he did so in the context of economic breakdown and as a critique of adventurism.

II. The Value-Price Transformation in Marx and the Problem of Crisis (1932)[287]

In reviews of *The Law of Accumulation*, Arkadij Gurland criticised Grossman for relying on Bauer's value schemas, while Hans Neisser accused him of ignoring the transformation of values into prices of production. Grossman's variations in his successive approximations, however, had dealt with these problems. One included merged departments, whereby values corresponded to prices. Grossman did this because he had been concerned with 'primarily general crises of overaccumulation that affect all spheres'.[288]

The problem of values and prices now had to be dealt with more thoroughly. Marx had already done so in the third volume of *Capital*, where his *value schema* had progressed, via the bridge of successive approximation, to a *prices of production schema*, thereby moving from the *general* (a model of capitalism as a whole) to the *particular* (prices of production for individual firms). Yet since Marx, the value schema had been treated as Marx's version of reality:

> Whether it is the neo-harmonists Kautsky, Hilferding and Otto Bauer, or Rosa Luxemburg and her followers, or finally Bukharin and other theorists of communism, all have treated the problem only at the level of its inception, by means of the value schema, which knows values, surplus value and different profit rates. Instead they should have substantiated their analyses and conclusions on the basis of a *production price schema*, which presents the regulating categories of prices of production, competition, and the average rate of profit... What could the analysis of a value schema possibly tell us about the necessary proportionality or disproportionality of commodity exchanges under capitalism when the proportional relationships so meticulously calculated in the value schema are later overturned by the tendency for profit rates to equalise and by the necessary redistribution of surplus value this causes!

Values and prices corresponded at a stage of small, pre-capitalist commodity production. Marx consistently stressed that this was no longer the case, even at the time of his writing, and that they now deviated permanently. He showed that while Ricardo and Smith developed a labour theory of value, they did so one-sidedly by claiming that commodities are sold at their values.

As the third volume of *Capital* makes clear, says Grossman, it is not values, assumed in theory,

> but the empirically given prices of production which form the objective centre of gravity around which everyday market prices oscillate. For concrete movements of capital, the empirically given general average rate of profit is decisively important...no such variation in the average rate of profit exists between different branches of production.

If commodities exchanged at their values, each capitalist would only benefit from the exploitation of the workers he employs and his profit would be identical to the surplus value that 'his' workers produce. Only the transformation of surplus value into the general rate of profit ensures 'that each individual capitalist, just like the totality of all capitalists...participates in the exploitation of the entire working class as a whole'.

The total surplus value circulating in a capitalist economy is a real quantity, but in the pure construction of the value schema, it is only accrued by productive capitalists, which are treated as one. Competition needs to be taken into account. Profit has to be divided into partial forms of profit: commercial profit, ground rent, money and bank capital all have to be deducted from productive capital. Nor can the existence of interest or interest rate movements be understood from the value schema.

> The rate of interest is related to the profit rate in a similar way as the market price of a commodity is to its value. In so far as the rate of interest is determined by the profit rate, this is always through the *general* rate of profit and not through the specific profit rates that may prevail in particular branches of industry...The general rate of profit, *in fact, reappears in the average rate of interest as an empirical, given fact.*

Prices of production 'are the regulator of the scope of production under capitalism, they determine the movement of capital, i.e. the steady injection and withdrawal of capital in individual spheres of production and, therefore, of the distribution of aggregate social capital'. Where industry is capital-intensive and produces low rates of profit, capitalists will shift their investment to something more labour intensive and profitable. But the more advanced capitalist development becomes, the more equalised the rate of profit in the individual spheres of production.

Luxemburg and Bauer, with their respective underconsumptionist and disproportionality theories, paid attention, says Grossman, 'only to categories which are unreal (different profit rates) and which – if they were realised – would inevitably [says Marx] "abolish…the entire system of capitalist production"!' Marx had said that 'empty tradition is more powerful in political economy than in any other science'. For Grossman, 'this is true not only of bourgeois economics but also, just as much, of the political economy of Marx's epigones'. Luxemburg and Bauer

> *from the outset exclude the necessity of transforming values first into prices of production and, further, into commercial prices from the circle of their problematic.*
>
> It is therefore only a logical consequence of this disastrous error that…not only the problem of the value-price transformation but also the connected problem of the *general rate of profit* and the problem of the transformation of surplus value into the *specific forms of profit* (commercial profit, interest, etc.), that is, *the whole theory of the third volume of Capital, do not exist!*

Luxemburg's interpretation of Marx's schema led her to the result that, without an average rate of profit, a sufficient amount of value could not be transferred from one department to another. This 'unsaleable remainder' in Department II is the source of her underconsumptionist breakdown theory.

Since competition leads to the transformation of values into prices of production and thus to a redistribution of surplus value among the individual branches of industry in the schema, which necessarily results in a modification of the previous relations of proportionality between the individual spheres of the schema, it is extremely possible and likely that a surplus of unsaleable consumer goods in the value schema subsequently vanishes in the production price schema and that, conversely, an original equilibrium in the value schema turns into disproportionality in the production price schema.

The tendency for profit rates to level out in different branches of production is an observation confirmed by experience and had been unanimously recognised before Marx. Marx refers to it as an 'empirical, given fact'. 'Observation of competition – the phenomena of production – shows that capitals of *equal* size yield an equal amount of profit on average.' The post-Ricardian school, which collapsed around 1850, could not reconcile the fact of a uniform rate of profit, however, with the labour theory of value. Grossman adds:

This is the point at which Marx's historical greatness became apparent. Through his theory of the divergence of prices of production from values, he was able to explain the fact of the uniform profit rate, which *prima facie* [on first appearances] contradicts the law of labour value, on the basis of this law of value.

III. Fifty Years of Struggle over Marxism 1883–1932 (1933)[289]

In 1933, Grossman wrote a valuable overview – one that perhaps only he could write – of the debates and developments that had taken place in Marxist economics since Marx's death. Referring to himself in the third person, he not only defended his theory of economics and revolution but emphasised his original contributions.

Grossman again attacked revisionism and reformism, associating these with the better-paid labour officials, a layer bolstered by the super-profits of imperialism, as Lenin had argued, and with an ambiguous relationship to the interests of the working class as a whole. Grossman also recognised that reformism had been strengthened with new expansions in production and, therefore, employment.[290]

In addition, Grossman moved on to the utopians who had tried to align Marx with the German philosopher Immanuel Kant. These neo-Kantians 'demanded a stronger consideration of "ideological" moments...and ethics in socialist theory'. Kant's starting point is the 'autonomous personality', 'a fundamental contradiction with socialism in general and Marxist socialism in particular, which only knows and explains individuals as conditioned by the social environment'.

Kautsky comes in for the most stick. Even before he turned away from revolution and breakdown theory, his Erfurt Programme, drawn up in 1891, which 'signified the highpoint' in the development of German social democracy,

> portrays the decisive point of the political programme very vaguely. The process of capitalist development seems to be the result of blind social forces. The conquest of power is wrapped in total darkness. The dictatorship of the proletariat [the rule of the working class] is not even mentioned. As a result, the political aspect of Marxism was virtually decapitated, until Lenin reconstructed it over 25 years later...However great Kautsky's service was in popularising Marxism, the real revolutionary character of Marxism remained alien to him.

Luxemburg, despite her mistaken theory, is recognised as a 'great fighter' who delivered some of the 'most impressive and enduring' essays, 'the highpoint' of which is her *Social Reform or Revolution*.

If Bernstein was expecting the transition to socialism [to result] from the progressive development of the bourgeois legal system, from statutory social reform, Luxemburg explains, then he was committing a fundamental error with regard to the essence of capitalist class rule. This rests, in contrast to earlier class societies, not on legally anchored 'acquired rights' but on real economic forces.

With 'the same acuity', Luxemburg 'develops her principal tactical ideas about the class struggle'. In praising this he again tacitly defends his own position on the way socialism has to be fought for (and shows why Liebknecht had been wrong to ignore Luxemburg).

For Marxism, trade union and political struggle is significant only as necessary preparation of the subjective factor in socialist upheaval – the working class – for the decisive revolutionary battle, first organising the workers 'as a class' and affecting the emergence of understanding, of united proletarian class consciousness. The socialist transition will not come of its own accord by fatalistically waiting for it to occur. It results, instead, from understanding, won in the everyday struggle of the working class, that the supersession of capitalism's objectively intensifying contradictions through social upheaval is indispensable. Thus for Luxemburg, as later for Lenin, reforms are only by-products of class struggle oriented on revolution. Revisionism, by contrast, makes everyday work independent of the final socialist goal. It separates reform from revolution and, by raising the movement to an end in itself, changes its character...This undialectical attitude sees only mutually exclusive opposites – either/or, reform or revolution – but not the subsumption of these opposites in the totality of the social process. [Luxemburg's interpretation of Marxism] assigns the decisive role to working class political activism, through the orientation of current work towards the final revolutionary goal, even though the seizure of state power is dependent on the objective course of material social development and 'presupposes...a definite degree of maturity of economic and political relations'. Marxism is therefore sharply distinguished from both fatalism and pure voluntarism.

Despite her mistaken theory, Luxemburg's assertion that 'the theory of capitalist collapse...is the cornerstone of scientific socialism' was 'the great historical significance' of her contribution, 'in conscious opposition to the attempted distortions of the neo-harmonists', who 'had to sail under the flag of Marxism' to deal with Marxism's popularity.

Her underconsumptionist theory of capitalist crisis was not new, though. It had been developed by Sismondi and Robert Malthus a century earlier and then extended by Heinrich Cunow, Louis B. Boudin and Kautsky. Luxemburg only differed in that she had used Marx's reproduction scheme to argue for the necessity of non-capitalist territories. The Narodniks in Russia, a voluntarist organisation, had adopted Sismondi's version of this theory. They had been rebuked by Lenin, but his own theory of crisis was based on the law of uneven development, i.e. disproportionality. Bukharin held up a breakdown theory,

but only speaks generally about the 'limit...given to a certain degree by the tension of capitalist contradictions' which 'will unavoidably lead to the collapse of capitalist rule', without proving this 'unavoidability'...Just as little does this interpretation provide concrete indicators by which the 'degree' of critical tension in the contradictions that make breakdown 'unavoidable' can be identified in advance. This can only be determined *ex post*, after the advent of the breakdown. Then, however, the theory of breakdown is superfluous as an instrument of scientific knowledge.

Grossman then was the first Marxist since Marx and Engels 'to support the theory developed by Marx, today almost forgotten'. He demonstrated that, for Marx, 'the decisive problem was not primarily partial crises arising from disproportionality but rather the primarily general crisis, "general glut", which is caused by "parallel production...which takes place simultaneously over the whole field"'. This glut of surplus capital is unprofitable to (re)invest and therefore a fetter on investment and productivity.

The classical economists had already correctly identified the tendency for the rate of profit to fall as a phenomenon but explained it as resulting from a supposed decline in the productivity of the soil. Marx and Grossman were the first to show that the falling rate of profit originated in the mode production, and fell inversely to the rising organic composition of capital.

Where, then, does the sudden *shift* to breakdown come from? Why can't capitalism survive with a rate of profit of 4% just as well as with one of 13-15%, as the declining rate is offset by a rising mass of profit?...

Grossman was the first to point out that breakdown cannot be derived from or explained by the *rate* of profit, that is by the index number of profits, but must be understood in terms of what is concealed behind it: the real *mass* of profit in relation to the social mass of capital. For, according to Marx, 'accumulation depends not only on the rate of profit but on the *amount* of profit'.

It is easy to calculate that with continuing accumulation

on the basis of an ever higher organic composition, a point must come when *all accumulation ceases*. This is all the more true because it is not any arbitrary fractional amount of capital that can be employed but rather a definite minimal amount is required, whose scale consistently grows with increasing accumulation of capital. With the progress of capital accumulation, therefore, an ever-larger part, not only absolutely but also relatively, must be deducted from surplus value for the purposes of accumulation. So at high levels of accumulation, when the extent of the total social capital is great, the part of surplus value required for additional accumulation, will be so large that it finally absorbs almost all of the surplus value. A point must be reached at which the part of surplus value destined for the consumption of the workers and the capitalists declines absolutely. That is the turning point at which the previously latent tendency to break down begins to take effect.

Grossman stresses that there are absolute limits to these counter-tendencies. Stocks, wages and commercial profits come up against definite points. The counter-effects of capital exports are also only temporary, as competition on the world market intensifies. 'For this reason too, the tendency to break down must become more intense, at a definite point.' The expansion in fixed capital, 'does not have a different effect. At higher levels of accumulation, at which fixed capital accounts for a larger component of constant capital, the contraction of production during the crisis has ever smaller significance: a firm's burden of depreciation and interest payments for fixed capital does not decline when production is reduced.'

It is, therefore,

apparent that the immanent laws of capital accumulation themselves progressively weaken the counter-tendencies.

Overcoming crises becomes ever more difficult, the tendency to break down more and more holds sway. The periods of upturn become ever shorter, the duration and intensity of crisis periods rises.

If crisis is, for [Grossman], the tendency to break down which has not fully developed, *the breakdown of capitalism is nothing other than a crisis that is not checked by counter-tendencies.*

For Marx, says Grossman, 'class struggle and revolution are inevitable concomitants of the immanent economic necessity with which development drives towards socialism. So capitalism approaches its end as a result of its inner economic laws.'

Not a single doubt is left about the importance of the proletariat taking political power through class struggle.

It is obvious to Grossman from the start that the question of perhaps fatalistically awaiting the 'automatic' breakdown without actively intervening, does not arise for the working class. Old regimes never 'fall' of their own accord, even during a period of crisis, if they are not 'toppled over' (Lenin). According to Grossman, the point of a Marxist theory of breakdown is only to demarcate voluntarism and putschism, which regard revolution as possible at any time without considering [whether there is] an objectively revolutionary situation and as dependent only on the subjective will of the revolutionaries. The point of breakdown theory is that the revolutionary action of the proletariat only receives its most powerful impetus from the objective convulsion of the established system and, at the same time, only this creates the circumstances necessary to successfully wrestle down ruling class resistance.

IV. Contributions to a Seminar Series on Monopoly Capitalism (1937)[291]

In 1936, Grossman contributed a succinct summary document on monopoly capitalism and its tendency towards total breakdown, published a year later, to an IfS seminar series. It confirmed something that remains somewhat taboo in the communist movement: Grossman's analysis of imperialism is better integrated into Marxist theory than Lenin's. Lenin only argued that the need to export surplus capital arose from the fact that '[a few capitalist countries] become "overripe" and (owing to the backward state of agriculture and the poverty of the masses) capital cannot find a field for "profitable" investment.'[292] While much of Lenin's work has been somewhat mistranslated, this does not offer anything like the clarity Grossman provides. The 'backward state of agriculture' – that it depends on permanent subsidies and destruction of produce due to the chronic overproduction that results in prices lower than the cost of production – is a prime example of overaccumulation.[293] The 'poverty of the masses' is also symptomatic of overaccumulation.

Varga, Bukharin, Hilferding and Bauer all argued that capital was exported only to obtain higher rates of profit, without explaining why or when (since, as Grossman explained in his book, when the newest technology is exported, the non-imperialist countries 'skip' phases of development and take on the highest possible organic composition).[294] Bauer even overlooked his own recognition that the formation of a world rate of profit led to unequal exchange in favour of countries with a higher organic composition. Luxemburg's theory was based on the oversaturation of consumption.

Only Grossman uncovered the roots of imperialism: capital became overabundant and therefore had to be invested overseas in order to expand the valorisation base and offset the resulting falling rate of profit. From this starting point he is able to clearly trace the development of monopoly capitalism through to its inevitable decline. Because the number of capital-exporting countries grows as capitalism ages,

> the number and extent of areas for investment, hence debtor countries, declines. The necessary result of this is a sharpening of the struggle for spheres of investment or the piling up of large quantities of unemployed capital, which eventually seeks valorisation in the unproductive spheres of the stock exchange and land speculation...it is precisely the struggle for spheres of investment which has led to wrongly directed capital investments, where no account has been taken of the given level of profitability, and which leads to collapses of the debtor countries.

The penetration of capital into new regions gives rise to new national economies, leading to a *structural* change in exports: 'Relatively, ever fewer finished commodities and more means of production are exported. That, however, requires ever more external markets.' Falling profitability is countered by taking on 'unbearable' debts which

> lead in increasing measure to a revolt of the debtor countries and the debtor strata against the creditor countries (and the creditor strata). Bankruptcies occur on a mass scale, demands are raised for moratoria and other interventions by the state, such as periodic [debt relief], but the impossibility of direct state intervention to the detriment of the creditors leads to the use of an indirect method of debt reduction: currency devaluation.

Ever-greater monopolies rise to offset falling profitability. They set excessively high prices and 'seek to reduce their own costs by exerting pressure on the prices of the raw materials and semi-finished goods they obtain from others'. A 'sharpening of the competitive struggle on the *world market'* initially remains 'limited to the *commodity aspect'* and 'conducted on the basis of a gold-backed currency which was regarded as...the holy of holies'.

The sharpening of competition proves to be insufficient, which is

> shown by the fact that now currencies are also brought into the conflict. The struggle among currencies, as the last available means of securing a price advantage in the competitive struggle, led to the abandonment of the gold standard and the automatic international balancing mechanism bound up with it...the splitting up of the world economy into individual, isolated regions, segregated from each other by tariff [tax] walls, compulsory currency regulations and quotas;...the destruction of the international credit system and of capital exports, and indeed to an inappropriate distribution of gold. The automatic international balancing mechanism was replaced by artificial balancing funds in individual states (currency manipulations).[295]

Currency manipulations

> should 'theoretically' contribute to *price stabilisation*, by raising prices, if prices are falling, and by reducing prices, if prices rise too steeply. Their actual meaning, however, is shown by the fact that in practice they function only *one-sidedly, in an inflationary direction*. At advanced levels of accumulation, where further open, direct pressure on wages meets with great resistance...these inflations and devaluations have the task of pushing through wage reductions in an indirect way.

Finally,

> a chronic excess of unemployed capital and a progressive increase in the unused capacity of heavy industry leads, despite all technological advances, to the destruction of great masses of capital and commodities and the reduction of the area under agricultural cultivation, and this at a time when vast numbers of unemployed people are not even sure of receiving the minimum required for existence. Capitalism has moved from its rising to its declining phase, in which the expansion of the productive forces of the economy is held back in the interests of the profits of a small minority of owners and to the detriment of the great mass of the people.

V. Marx, Classical Political Economy and the Problem of Dynamics (1941)[296]

Dissatisfied with the dominant view that Marx 'completed' the work of the classical economists, Grossman wanted to show that Marx had thoroughly critiqued it to the point of opposing their politics and 'revolutionisng' the foundations of economic thought. In contrast to the static character of political economy, only Marxism could explain the dynamic restructurings of the economy as capitalism aged. Against theories of equilibrium and limitless accumulation, Marx demonstrated that capitalist development tended towards increasing *disequilibrium* and, eventually, a final collapse.

For Marx, classical economy was followed by three phases of 'vulgar economics'. The former embodied the industrial capitalists when they were revolutionary. Ricardo's labour theory of value underpinned his theory of ground rent. The former was therefore useful at such a time because it could be directed against the landlords and usurers as unproductive parasites eating into industrial profits and thereby holding back societal progress.

Once the proletariat, however, became numerically significant and its theoretical representatives drew egalitarian and socialist conclusions from Ricardo's labour theory of value – the right of the working class to the full fruits of its labour – political economy began to regress. The new industrial and old land-owning rulers compromised on the basis of their shared anti-proletarian interests. The distinctions between productive and unproductive labour were abandoned. Ricardo's labour theory of value is replaced by the conception that all labour is equally productive; his theory of ground rent with the theory that consumption is necessary to overcome overproduction. Gradually the labour theory of value is transformed into a 'meaningless' theory of costs of production. Labour is only acknowledged as a factor of production alongside land and capital.

In the third period, the remaining acknowledged contradictions are erased and accumulation now drinks from the fountain of youth: it is postulated as harmonious and inexhaustible. The idea that it could ever collapse under the weight of its own contradictions – or be overthrown by an excluded social majority – is treated as an absurdity. Finally, after mass uprisings in 1848, all genuine theory is abandoned and replaced with the empirical description of phenomena.

Under the scrutiny of Ricardian socialists, even the costs of production theory had to be replaced by a subjective theory of value. Labour becomes not an objective expenditure of energy measured by time but a psychological sacrifice. 'In order for capital to be granted equal status with labour as a parallel factor in the creation of value, it must also be turned into a psychological variable,' says Grossman. 'If the wage is the reward for the effort of labour then the interest on capital is the reward for the subjective sacrifice of saving, the renunciation of immediate consumption of capital.'

Because Marx revives the labour theory of value, the

Ricardian socialists regard him as deriving socialist conclusions from Ricardo. By uncovering the dual character of wage labour, capital and the commodity, Marx does much more than that. The classical economists thought equal labour times always exchange for equal labour times, including the exchange relation between the worker and the entrepreneur. They thought they had grasped the deceptive appearance of phenomena, but only did so with the appearance of money and in terms of labour in general, rather than the specific epoch of wage labour, which gives the appearance that the worker's labour is fully compensated. The illusion is really due to the (exchange) value form in general. It self-evidently cannot arise from use-value, for a commodity's utility is transparent.

'Because capitalism has a dual reality, mystifying and non-mystifying sides, and binds them together in a concrete unity, any theory which reflects this reality must likewise be a unity of opposites,' says Grossman. Specific forms of labour create specific use-values, but labour in general creates exchange-value.

We find ourselves here at the real centre of Marx's innovation. The great significance of the new conception is that Marx found in it a means of eliminating what was deceptive in the pure categories of exchange-value and thus created a foundation for his further research into capitalist production, which gave him the possibility of grasping the true interconnections of this production, behind the veil of value.

Marx's two-sided approach revealed capitalism's crisis tendency. Fixed capital naturally lasts longer than circulating capital (cash, operating expenses, raw materials, etc.) and is therefore replaced in a completely different manner…on one hand as value and on the other as use-value… Marx derived the necessity of periodic crises already under simple reproduction, from this difference in the mode of replacement.

The unity of opposites is apparent again in the falling rate of profit, between the inverse movement of the mass of use-values and values.

The richer a society, the greater the development of labour's productive power, the larger the volume of useful things which can be made in a given labour time. At the same time, however, the value of these things becomes smaller. The greater the mass of use-values, the more pronounced the tendency for the rate of profit to fall (in value terms).

For Ricardo, market prices oscillated around 'natural' values, meaning disequilibrium is caused only by external forces (wars, bad harvests, state intervention). His 'deceleration and cessation of capital accumulation in the distant future' therefore has to be described as 'pseudo-dynamics' as 'the "dynamic" factor is not inherent in the economic process'.

Marxism, however, explains the dynamic structural changes in the economy as capitalism develops, while bourgeois theory, focusing almost exclusively on distribution and consumption, takes on a static character, based on theories of equilibrium whereby supply matches demand, or vice-versa, implying limitless accumulation.

Marginal utility theory, the delinquent offspring of subjective value theory, is even more abstract. Dealing only in quantities and disregarding any qualitative content, it is pure metaphysics. Production is governed by subjective demand. The theory does not account for the fact that 'economic phenomena are in motion and must therefore be dealt with in units of time'. Equilibrium is achieved if two people possessing a certain number of goods exchange them with each other on the market until both parties agree that no further exchange is possible. The state of equilibrium attained is therefore defined as indefinite if there is no change in conditions or if this change is so slight that the system self-corrects.

All the quantities of goods or prices are received as increments by others. 'Hence all these (positive or negative) increments in the number of goods or prices result in a total sum of zero... They are transfers, a timeless "movement", a circular motion...' Dynamic structural changes have to be explained away 'as mere "oscillations" around a state of equilibrium or as temporary "disturbances" prior to the achievement of a new equilibrium'.

Crisis is explained only by the mismanagement of the money supply, which can be stabilised by changing the interest rate. But credit expansion/contraction is a dependent variable. An underproduction of surplus value or an amount of capital tied up in circulation creates an impulse to expand credit. Grossman points out that Marx was able to explain this by creating all the categories and concepts of circulation which were connected with the previously neglected time element. There is no basis for any accusation that Marx focused one-sidedly on production. Instead of equilibrium,

reality demonstrates long term disequilibrating movements... The concept of 'self-regulation' serves to divert attention away from the actually prevailing chaos of the destruction of capital, the bankruptcy of entrepreneurs and factories, mass unemployment, insufficient capital investment, currency disturbances, and arbitrary redistributions of property. Only in this way is the introduction into economic theory of concepts of 'statics' and 'dynamics', which originated in theoretical physics, without any justification of such a twofold division of theory, understandable.

Marx's conception of the dual character of all economic phenomena 'compelled him to look at the economy in its specific movement, not statically'. He found that equilibrium is only possible under the unrealistic assumption that all values and technological developments are constant. The distinction between the lifetimes of fixed and circulating capital had not been made before, and revealed disequilibrium even in simple reproduction.

While raw materials have to be renewed annually, fixed capital (e.g. 2000 units in Department II) lasts for several years. Department II does not need to buy any fixed capital from Department I during this time. Since, however, the annual productive capacity of Department I remains 2000 units, overproduction – an unsaleable remainder – must necessarily take place in Department I, despite reproduction on a constant scale. 'Normal' production could then only take place in Department I if (despite the assumption of simple reproduction in Department I) Department II expands over several years. 'This is, however, impossible. For the faster expansion of department II, on the basis of the given technology, presupposes an impossible increase in the working population.' Rather than demand creating its own matching supply, overproduction reigns.

Grossman again laments that the Marxist literature has regarded the problem of equilibrium exclusively from its value dimension. There have to be certain quantitative value proportions in both departments of the reproduction schemes if all the quantities of value supplied and demanded are to be exchanged without a remainder. The analysis of the material side of the labour process was reduced to the single proposition that in the process of reproduction, Department I must produce means of production and Department II means of consumption. Marx's conception of equilibrium, however, includes 'quite definite technical proportions that must exist between the mass of labour and the mass of the means of production'.

In simple reproduction, the process supplies the same mass of use-values and satisfies the same quantity of needs in both the current and the previous year. So even if a bad harvest reduced the amount of cotton by half, for example, resulting in each unit of cotton costing double, a 'market equilibrium' remains in terms of value. The technical side would be halved, though, because spindles and looms would have to be shut down. Yet 'because too much has been produced, there is an impulse to produce still more!' since capitalists are compelled to reduce prices through innovation and expansion if they are to withstand competition. The mass of use-values rises but the profit rate falls. 'Under such circumstances equilibrium...can only occur... by chance within the general irregularity, as a momentary point of transition in the midst of constant disequilibrium.'

The indicated direction of this course 'encounters a limit and approaches its end' because 'the degree of the progressive maturation of concrete labour can only be expressed in its value, in the fall of the rate of profit...a symptom of the approaching supersession of capital's rule'. The marginal, limitless accumulation of capital is not possible, and credit cannot be controlled. Grossman quotes Marx:

> The decrease in the interest rate is therefore a symptom of the annulment of capital only inasmuch as it is a symptom of the growing domination of capital in the process of perfecting itself – of the estrangement which is growing and therefore hastening to its annulment.[297]

VI. The Evolutionist Revolt against Classical Political Economics (1943)[298]

'The Evolutionist Revolt against Classical Political Economics' complemented *Dynamics* in its rejection of another myth about Marx's role in the history of political economy – laying to rest the dominant misconception that Marx had been the first to argue that history developed along the lines of successive modes of production. By reclaiming Marx's real originality, Grossman rebuked the critics of his own theory of progress and revolution.

In examining Marx's predecessors, Grossman showed how 'dynamic or evolutionary thinking actually entered the field of economics', something that had 'not been adequately or at all accurately presented in our economic literature'. The 'sociologising' of history had been 'falsely attributed' to the German philosopher Georg Wilhelm Friedrich Hegel (1770-1831). Marx too had been subsequently credited, by Werner Sombart, with sociologising economics and creating the concept of the economic system, an achievement the hardly shy Marx himself never claimed. Instead, says Grossman, the French and English economists, not the German, had laid the basis for modern evolutionary theories of economics, 'and particularly for the work of Marx'.

Sombart's view had been echoed in socialist circles. Eduard Heimann said Marx was the first to 'historicise' capitalism as a transient mode of production, something he was able to do as the 'heir' of Hegel. In fact, whereas most theorists of the French enlightenment (1688-1789) 'held the philosophical view that history was an endless progress marking man's path to reason' – albeit based on a rational 'natural order' from nature and without revolutions – Hegel believed history had ended in his own day, thanks to the mediating role that state administration and civic institutions play in preventing revolutionary social conflict. For Hegel, 'the historical process thus becomes a glorification of the history of the middle classes', says Grossman. Hegel also rejected the concept that 'a higher, more developed phase proceeds from the preceding, lower phase'. Hegel's original contribution had been to focus on the essence of development, but he did so in the sphere of idealism – of logic and consciousness – rather than material history.

The classical political economists, including Smith and Ricardo, spoke only about one and the same capitalist society progressing towards post-scarcity.

All previous societies were measured with the yardstick of free trade...they knew of only two ideal states: the 'original state of things', occurring before the fall from grace, as it were, and the bourgeois state...All intervening epochs...were never discussed in terms of the limitations and conditions of their own time.

From the late eighteenth century, though, theorists outside the mainstream in France and England 'based their universal laws and predictions on *history*' and 'observed evolutionary tendencies'. They had witnessed the French Revolution and so eternal natural laws evidently could not apply to social science, the task of which is to 'seek the law of change itself'.

Isolated individuals during the Middle Ages and Renaissance (Vico) had been concerned with the evolutionary idea. But it did not become a current of thought until the last third of the eighteenth century or triumphant until the first half of the nineteenth century. The six men who represented this current were the Frenchmen Marie-Jean-Antoine-Nicolas de Condorcet (1743-94), Henri Saint-Simon (1760-1825) and Sismondi (1773-1842); the Englishmen James Stueart (1712-1825) and Reverend Richard Jones (1790-1855); and Marx, 'who synthesised and completed the whole development'.

The pioneer of the new approach, Condorcet, understood the French Revolution only through 'revolutions which preceded and prepared the way for it'. For Grossman, he introduced 'the idea of natural laws of historical development and the collectivist view of history as a history of the masses'.

Saint-Simon sought to give history 'the strictly scientific

character that marked astronomy and chemistry'. He recognised that the strongest determining factor in all social change is not the spiritual element but the productivity of social labour and the organisation of property and class relations. The legislative superstructure is determined by the economic base, changes in which lead to revolutionary crises. The class which controls production must rise to the position of society's ruling political class. While he did not condemn capitalism, he saw the industrial working class, the 'only useful' class, increasingly outnumbering the other classes and so thought 'it must end by becoming the only class'. There would eventually be no need for government, only for administration.

Stueart added inductive (empirical) investigation to the deductive method of Ricardo in his explanation of capitalism's supersession of feudalism. The 'sociologising of economic categories and institutions was carried through still more systematically' by Jones. Testing existing theories against actual developments, he exposed the classical idea that capital formed primitively through 'savings' when it had done so through the expropriation of peasants.

The decisive factor for Jones in differentiating systems is the way in which human labour is organised. As this factor changes, so does the whole economic system. On a historical materialist basis, he developed the idea that nations must pass through a sequence of economies, at varying tempos. The intellectual and moral character of a country is conditioned by the economic structure; and the superstructure reacts back on the productive capacities of the base. Like Sismondi, he thought capitalism was dependent on a consuming class and foresaw a future socialised form of production. The two were ignored by the classical school and did not gain any recognition again until Marx.

By combining the work of the evolutionists with elements of Hegel's philosophy of history, Marx 'created an integrated, original theory'. Unlike his predecessors, who only generalised development on the basis of particular observations, Marx, like Hegel,

> understood the relationship between the particular and the universal quite differently, viewing the historical 'object' as made up not of individual observations but of the 'cultural whole' of social-collective unities. Using the genetic method of the dialectic, with its constant creation and synthesis of opposites, Marx sought to grasp the evolution of these collective unities in their historical necessity. Every present moment contains both the past, which has led to it logically and historically, and the elements of further development in the future.
>
> ... In other words, history has not a relativistic character, it does not depend on the accident of the observer's point of view, ideals, or standards. What Marx did was to remove the study of history from that subjective level to a higher one, where objective, measurable stages of development are perceived. He fulfilled Saint-Simon's hope of making history a science.

By also drawing on Charles Darwin's emphasis on the 'technology' of nature, i.e. the formation of organs of plants and animals as instruments to explain the origin and development of species, Marx also identifies each historical period's objective tendencies from the nature of the technological instruments used by the social organisation of labour. The close link between history and theory 'distinguished Marx from his predecessors'. As opposed to the static approach of the classicists, 'Marx is the spokesman of the new dynamic approach'.

Although Marx produced 'profound' assessments of each epoch, his efforts were focused on socialism's succession of capitalism, which he saw as a 'process of *natural history*' (Engels).[299] Within the existing economy a new economic form objectively arises and grows. The superstructure resists the demands made by the new base and the two enter into an ever-sharper conflict. Through violent resolution the new economy finally takes over. The subjective bearer of this change is the class struggle and political revolution, which establishes a new, applicable superstructure. Marx provided the sound economic theory lacking in his predecessors. 'When the process of accumulation reaches a certain point...all further accumulation of capital will become impossible,' says Grossman. 'The basis will have been laid for great political and economic transformations.'

Like Grossman, Marx had 'frequently been charged with a "fatalistic" theory of the "historical necessity"' of socialism. Yet in

all his writings Marx characteristically emphasises the unity of theory and practice. This so-called 'historical necessity' does not operate automatically but requires the active participation of the working class in the historical process. This participation, however, is itself not something arbitrary but follows from the pressure of the objective factors. The student of history and the forward-looking practical politician must therefore consider this subjective factor as in fact another objective condition of the historical process.

'No predecessor of Marx had a similar theory.' While Saint-Simon and his school

do not give the working class any political role in the transformation of society, the main result of Marx's doctrine is the clarification of the historical role of the proletariat as the carrier of the transformative principle and the creator of the socialist society...In changing the historical *object*, the *subject* changes himself...Only through these struggles does the working class change and re-educate itself and become conscious of itself.

Those who had attributed to Marx the first application of evolutionary thinking reduced his historical contributions 'to a level that does not go beyond the horizon of bourgeois liberalism; that is, beyond the idea of evolution in the direction of constant progress "from the incomplete to the complete" – to quote Hegel'.

Chapter 5

The Final Breakdown

The Covid-19 lockdowns sparked the greatest economic crash in capitalist history. In just 22 trading days, the S&P 500 stock market in the US (measuring the value of the richest 500 US companies) fell by 30% from a record high on 19 February 2020 – the fastest ever slump of such magnitude. The second, third and fourth took place in 1934, 1931 and 1929, respectively.[300]

This crisis, however, is much worse. Official US national debt in 1929 stood at 16% of GDP; 44% at the start of WWII; and 65% before the Great Recession – after which it exploded to 104%.[301] Although it hit 121% at the end of WWII, it has been almost as high since 2009, without the impact of a world war. In the second quarter of 2020, it hit a record 136%.

In 2013, gross national debt and household debt (85% of GDP) hit record highs at the same time for the first time ever.[302] The US stock market during the Great Depression fell to its lowest point in 1932, a decline of nearly 89% compared to the high point in 1929. The worst is yet to come.

The Covid-19 lockdowns – suiting monopoly capital's need for depressed prices and wages; and the destruction of small, medium and surplus capital – exacerbated the depth of the recession but played the role of catalyst rather than cause. With stocks overinflated in value, at 150% of GDP, they were extremely vulnerable to an external shock. Stocks would not have tumbled by 30% if an epic bubble had not already formed.

Official aggregate global debt (of governments, corporations and households), already at 200% of world GDP *before* 2008, continues to hit new heights, indicating a record-high overaccumulation of capital in relative as well as absolute terms. In June 2019, the International Monetary Fund (IMF) said global debt stood at an official $184 trillion, 225% of world GDP. This averages out at $86,000 for every person, 2.5 times the global average annual per capita income. By some estimates, though, once 'off-the-books' net obligations such as social security are taken into account, official figures are understated by a factor of 2.5, making actual global debt (as of July 2019) $460 trillion, 560% of GDP and $215,000 per person; and the US figure not 105%, but 390%.[303] If that is the case, then the true number is even higher. The IMF calculation only includes households, governments and non-financial corporates, whereas the Institute of International Finance (IIF) also includes the outstanding debt of financial institutions (and is more frequently updated). The IIF put global debt in the third quarter of 2017 at $233 million, 327% of GDP.

It said gross debt issuance hit an 'eye-watering' record of $12.5 trillion in the second quarter of 2020 compared with a quarterly average of $5.5 trillion in 2019, with some 60% of new issues coming from governments. The IIF said global debt reached a new peak of $253 trillion in the third quarter of 2019, 322% of world GDP, up from $244 trillion and 318% year-on-year. That was *before* the lockdowns. At the end of 2020, the figures surged to $281 trillion and 355%.

In 2015, global debt was estimated to be 2.5 times higher than the global money supply, 25% higher than just 2 years earlier.[304] This is despite the fact that the US monetary base (which discounts credit and reserves) shot up from $847bn in July 2008 to $2.1 trillion in February 2010 and then $4 trillion in September 2014. After dipping to $3.2 trillion in September 2019, it catapulted to $5.1 trillion in June 2020.[305] As of 23 November 2020, *21% of all US dollars had been printed in 2020, taking the figure to 75% over the past 12 years*, sparking fears about monetary financing, which is historically associated with hyperinflation.

The US monetary stock (which includes credit and reserves) has grown *even faster*. It surged from $7.5 trillion at the start of

2008 to $12.4 trillion at the end of 2015; and then again from $15.33 trillion at the end of 2019 to $18.3 trillion at the end of July 2020 (by more than 23% year-on-year, easily beating the previous record of 15%).[306]

The quantity of *negative*-yielding sovereign (national) debt – which barely existed before 2014 – hit $14 trillion in the first half of 2019, $15 trillion at the start of August and $16.7 trillion before the end of the month. In the middle 2 weeks of August 2019 the proliferation of negative-yielding bonds erupted – 30% of global, tradeable bonds were being sold at a guaranteed loss. In December 2020, the figure hit $18 trillion. Earlier in the year, the British government sold bonds at negative yields for the first time ever. Spain and Australia followed. Michael Pento, author of *The Coming Bond Market Collapse*, has said since writing his book in 2013 that,

Not even I would ever have fantasised there could ever be trillions of dollars of negative yielding sovereign debt and even negative yielding corporate debt…Governments are borrowing money and paying you back no interest and less than your principal payment. That has never before happened in the history of the world…But it's not just happening in the US. It's a global bubble.[307]

Although most private debt has been socialised, heaped onto the backs of the global working class, it is now simply too large to work off – it must be destroyed. Pento has compared the situation to the end of the Roman Empire.[308]

Essentially, the private sector is becoming almost entirely dependent on the state subsidies and orders – but, in turn, the state is becoming almost entirely dependent on central bank monetary financing.

The pre-2020 decline

That the next crash was looming before the events beginning in late-2019 is undeniable. The 'recovery' from the Great Recession had been the weakest since WWII. Whereas US GDP grew by 43% over the first 39 quarters of the 1991-2001 expansion, in the first 39 quarters of the last expansion, up to March 2019, it grew by only 22%. At that rate, the last expansion would have had to continue for another 6 years to equal the aggregate growth of 1991-2001, and 9 more years to match the 54% recorded over the 1961-69 expansion.[309]

Corporate profits peaked in 2015. Trump's record corporate tax cut in 2017 – from 35% to 21% – saw after-tax profit rates resume an upward turn, but the promised 3-6% growth did not materialise (averaging 2.4% between the end of 2017 and the end of 2019). Corporate tax receipts in 2019 were down by 23% compared to 2 years earlier.

In August 2019, the US yield curve inverted for the first time since 2007. That is, the interest rate (yield/return) on 10-year government bonds (loans to the government) fell below the rate on the 2-year equivalent. At the time, 2-year Treasuries Bills (T-Bills) were trading at a yield (return) of 1.634%, while 10-year T-Bills only offered 1.628%. The longer-dated debt should normally offer a better rate of return, as there is simply more time for something to go wrong before the money is due to be repaid and investors need short-term returns to pay short-term bills and expenses. Inverted yield curves therefore imply that investors have become more pessimistic about growth.

August 2019 updates also revealed that Germany's economy had contracted by 0.1% in the second quarter, while Britain's shrank by 0.2%. Germany's yield curve inversion was worse than in the US and Britain. Berlin responded with an auction of €2bn of new 30-year bonds at 0%, meaning it would simply take money and promise to return it in 2049. Inflation, of course, could have eroded much of its value by then, making conditions very difficult for insurance firms and pension and hedge fund managers whose job it is to grow their clients' wealth.

That the US yield curve inversion happened *after* a base interest rate cut, from 2.25% to 2% at the end of July 2019, was described by Pento as 'very remarkable'. But the remarkable kept coming. While falling share and rising bond prices in a crisis usually generate falling interest rates – since government debt is 'safer', on the basis that the state can print money – on 9 March 2020 the 10-year US Treasury Bond interest rate spiked upwards. According to one bond trader, 'statistically speaking, [this] should only happen every few millennia'.[310] Even when the giant 160-year-old investment bank Lehman Brothers went bankrupt in September 2008, this did not happen.

The Fed pledged asset purchases with no limit to support markets, taking the unprecedented action of buying up corporate bonds and exchange-traded investment funds in the primary market. (In the secondary market, proceeds from the sale of bonds go to the counterparty, say an investor or a dealer; whereas in the primary market, money from investors goes directly to the issuer.) This happened because, after 9 March, corporate interest rates surged so high that few corporations could borrow money at any price. Investors were refusing to lend to them, meaning corporations faced a credit crunch – despite global sovereign negative interest rates.

The Fed has prevented a deflation in asset prices in order to keep, for example, pension funds afloat. As of 29 February 2020, the Fed held $2.47 trillion, 14.6%, of $16.9 trillion marketable US Treasury securities outstanding, making it by far the largest single holder of US Treasuries anywhere in the world. By the end of March, this rose by an unprecedented monthly increase of $650bn, to $3.12 trillion. One estimate said that if this pace of buying continued, the Fed would 'own the entire Treasury market in about 22 months'.[311] Pento, one of the few bourgeois pundits to have warned of the Great Recession, argues that:

They're going to reinflate junk [high-risk] bond prices again. They'll exceed the 2% inflation target greatly. All bond yields will rise inexorably, prices will crash. And then the Fed will have nothing they can do. There will be no relief package coming from any government on the planet. No tax base can cope with that amount of debt. You cannot resolve an inflation crisis, you cannot placate a market that is rising, with cratering prices, by creating more inflation; or by borrowing more funds into existence. You can't do it. That's the real crash that's coming.[312]

Automation and the falling rate of profit

That capitalism is unsustainable has long been empirically observable. Most obviously, manufacturing costs and commodity prices, despite inflation and rising indirect taxes, have been trending towards zero. As Marx and Grossman argued, as the mass of use-values rises, the price per unit falls, compelling capitalists to continually intensify the contradiction. For example, whereas the world's fastest supercomputer in 1975 commanded a price of $5m ($32m in 2013's money), an iPhone 4 released in 2010 with the equivalent performance could be bought for $400. Aerospace companies producing engines in 2010 for $24m in 24 months are now 3-D (three-dimensional) printing them for $2000 in 2 weeks. Furthermore, rather than having globalised supply chains, such companies foresee the entire product being built in 'at home'.[313] While 'offshoring' manufacturing jobs to the 'low-income economies' saves up to 65% on labour costs, replacing human workers with robots saves up to 90%.[314]

While industrialisation, particularly in Asia, saw 83 'developing countries' achieve growth rates by the early 2000s that were more than twice the rate of the 'developed' world, the rest of the world has seen the same opportunity end 'prematurely' (discounting any Luxemburgist theory of the approaching final crisis). Even Latin America and Sub-Saharan Africa have been deindustrialising in the past decade – from a much lower starting point than Asia.[315] Whereas industrialisation peaked in western European countries at income levels of around $14,000, India and many sub-Saharan African countries appear to have reached their peak manufacturing employment at income levels of $700 (both at 1990 levels).[316]

Not only do robots and 3-D-printing increasingly remove the incentive for capitalists to invest overseas, the incentive to exploit international transit workers – with self-driving vehicles having the same effect – is also disappearing. The economic relation that underpins imperialism is unravelling.

Similarly, the emergence of cellular agriculture (lab-grown food), with falling prices and rising quality, is estimated to see the beef industry go bust by 2035.[317] And whereas the first example of Human Genome Sequencing – which, in line with socialist principles, is set to revolutionise health care by making it preventative – required 13 years and billions of dollars, it now takes under an hour and could cost 'as little as flushing a toilet' by 2022.[318]

Clearly, the quicker and more automated commodity production becomes, the closer capitalism gets to its final breakdown. As James Manyika, McKinsey Global Institute director, said in June 2017: 'Find a factory anywhere in the world built in the past 5 years – not many people work there.'

Services jobs are increasingly automated, too. In 2018 Goldman Sachs said, for example, that a trading desk occupied by 500 people 15-20 years ago is now staffed by three. In Britain, the number of supermarket checkout assistants fell by 25.3% between 2011 and 2017.[319]

At the end of March 2020, after most countries had entered lockdowns, almost half of company bosses in 45 countries said they were speeding up the implementation of automation.[320] With lockdown turning the home into a more common place of work, Microsoft could boast of having discovered a fresh way of reducing costs (by pushing bills onto workers) and extending absolute labour time as it announced 'two years' worth of digital transformation in two months'.[321] As *The Guardian* reported at the end of April:

> Bank branches were already closing in droves, but here is the perfect excuse to shut more. The authors of an Oxford University study thought that by 2035 it would be possible to automate 86% of restaurant jobs, three-quarters of retail jobs, and 59% of recreation jobs. By unlucky coincidence, those are among the very industries hardest hit by an epidemic now demanding quantum leaps in efficiency if some companies are to avoid going under.[322]

But automation is abolishing the source of profit – capital's exploitation of commodity-producing labour. To be more precise, automation is the final expression of capitalism's self-abolishing tendency. This is reflected empirically: according to estimates by Esteban Maito, the general rate of profit in the 'high-income countries' fell overall from a decade average of 43% in the 1870s to 17% in the 2000s. As of 2014, it is on course to reach zero around 2054. As Marx wrote in *Grundrisse*, published in 1858:

> As soon as labour in the direct form has ceased to be the great wellspring of wealth, labour time ceases and must cease to be its measure...Capital thus works towards its own dissolution as the form dominating production.[323]

But this dissolution is not expressed by the rate of profit drifting seamlessly downwards to zero, since capital does not accumulate harmoniously and, at some point, becomes too large for the relatively dwindling pool of workers to valorise.

While Grossman does not address automation specifically, he points out that the ratio of mechanisation to labour tends to rise regardless of the mode of production. Under capitalism the trend towards fully automated production is driven primarily by the demands of accumulation – its ever-greater need to raise productivity – but it is also a historical trend. Fully automated production cannot be consummated under capitalism, though, since the system will necessarily break down beforehand.

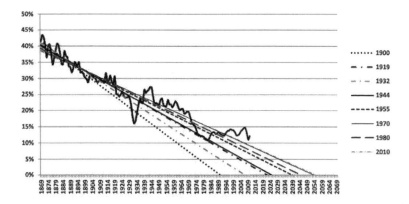

The general rate of profit falls historically towards zero, meaning capitalism must end. Source: Estaban Maito

Absolute overaccumulation

Whereas the neo-harmonists thought that the rate of profit 'could tend downwards indefinitely, getting closer and closer to zero without ever disappearing altogether',[324] Grossman stressed that: 'There is an absolute limit to the accumulation of capital and this limit comes into force much earlier than a zero rate of profit.'[325]

He said it was 'completely false' to assert that only in the case of a zero rate of profit 'can we speak of an absolute overaccumulation of capital', that 'as long as capital yields a profit, however small, we cannot speak of overaccumulation in an absolute sense because the capitalist would rather be content

with a small profit than have no profit at all'.[326] Grossman goes
on:

> In identifying the conditions on which this limit depends,
> mere empiricism is quite useless. For instance in the utilisation
> of fuel the experience of almost 100 years has shown that it
> was always possible to obtain a greater quantity of heat from
> a given quantity of coal. Thus experience, based on several
> decades' practice, might easily suggest that there is no limit
> to the quantity of heat obtainable through such increases.
> Only theory can answer the question whether this is really
> true, or whether there is not a maximum limit here beyond
> which any further increases are precluded. This answer is
> possible because theory can calculate the absolute quantity
> of energy in a unit of coal. Increases in the rate of utilisation
> cannot exceed 100% of the available quantity of energy.
> Whether this maximum point is reached in practice is of no
> concern to theory.[327]

The same logic is applicable to capital accumulation, which
tends to grow absolutely, and its source, human labour power.
As coal is converted into heat, 'living labour' is converted into
the 'dead labour' of fixed capital. In a very material sense, all
of the exploited labour ever expended has paved the way to
socialism.

In *Capital*, Marx points out that the surplus labour time of
the working class as a whole cannot be extended indefinitely.[328]
A growing amount of investment is needed just to keep the
same number of people or even fewer employed. Capital cannot
even afford to exploit an ever-increasing part of the working
class, surplus labour that grows alongside surplus capital.
Those who do retain employment are increasingly pressed into
low-productivity services work or unproductive work in the
commercial sector, the fastest growing sector across the world.

Absolute overaccumulation first applies in a country when increased investment produces the same or less surplus value than before. Profits are still being made, but additional investment is pointless. The country is then compelled to export capital. As we have seen, though, there is a limit to capital exports. The world's labour supply is not bottomless – and deindustrialisation is now a global phenomenon. Additional capital exports are also becoming pointless. *Capital is exhausting its own ability to expand its valorisation base.* Reproduction can now only tend to contract. Imperialism as an economic relation is in retreat.

Another definite limit to the counter-tendencies is the lowering of interest rates, a 'symptom of the annulment of capital', as Marx said.

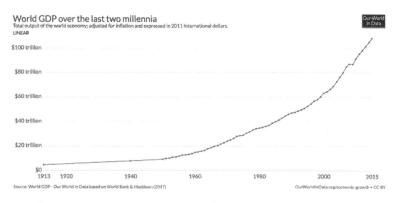

The ever-steepening trajectory of accumulation indicates the eventual inevitability of an absolute historical limit.

Converging empirical limits

Empirically, there are several approaching economic limits that cannot be converging at the same time merely by coincidence. Average GDP growth rates in what the World Bank defines as 'high income countries' are already closing in on zero, having fallen every decade apart from the last one for the past half century: from 5.59% in the 1960s, to 4.15% in the 1970s; 2.93% in the 1980s; 2.35% in the 1990s; and 1.78% in the 2000s. The figure rose slightly to 2.1% in the 2010s, but this minor reprieve, based on murderous austerity measures and record levels of debt, has already proven to be unsustainable.[329]

As well as being propped up by debt, GDP in the imperialist nations is inflated by the profits leeched from the 'developing world'. Productivity growth in the high-income countries, since 2011, has spluttered below 1%.

After the crash of March 2020, interest rates were reduced to cheapen the cost of borrowing in Britain and the US from 0.75 and 1.5% to 0.1 and 0.25% respectively. Since 1958, lifting the US economy out of recession has taken an average cut of 6%. While going deep into negative rates might be tolerated for a while – the alternative to losing some of an investment is to lose most or all of it by letting the banking system collapse – they would at some point disincentivise bond buying. Even if converting cash into stocks were to be compelled by bail-ins and taxes on wealth and cash – to bring down the rates on long-term debt – there is a definite limit to the amount of convertible physical cash, which only makes up about 1% of all US dollars. The rest is in the form of electrons stored in a bank server or brokerage account. The banks don't have trillions in physical dollar bills lying around in vaults – a physical impossibility – to meet redemptions if people start demanding their money in actual physical cash (when investors sell stocks they effectively 'buy cash').

Either way, rates will eventually have to turn back upwards, at some point sparking the greatest debt panic in history.[330] Debt-to-GDP will surge yet higher and the tax base will continue to shrink – the US government's ability to meet its debt obligations will become all but impossible. Bondholders will realise that what they are owed cannot be repaid and increasingly transfer their funds into hard assets, especially precious metals, reinforcing inflation.

After the introduction of a record $3 trillion bailout package to keep businesses afloat during the lockdown, the official US national debt hit £26.5 trillion, 123% of GDP. The annual deficit – the difference between government income and expenditure – is expected to have ballooned from $984bn in 2019 to $3.8 trillion in 2020. That's 18% of GDP, flying up from 3.8% in September 2019; and twice as high as its worst point following the Great Recession. The US has never defaulted on more than a small part of its debt but, historically, countries that have failed to get their debt-to-GDP back below 90% have gone bankrupt and defaulted on their debt as a whole, forcing them to go cap in hand to the IMF for a bailout (usually in the form of high-interest loans and on the condition of privatising state assets and public services). These, though, have been relatively small economies. Given that the US dollar is the world's reserve currency, the IMF effectively *is* the US.

In 2011, Treasury Secretary Timothy Geithner told Congress that a US government default would cause interest rates to spike the world over because US Treasury bonds represent the benchmark borrowing rate and investors would no longer be as sure of future payment.[331] If the government defaulted and either refused to pay interest or said it would pay bonds back at a fraction of the face value, trillions of dollars in what were previously safe assets would be wiped out. In such an event, Geithner said the US government may have to stop paying salaries to soldiers and state officials.

As profits become more and more stagnant and debt more onerous, an increasing number of capitalists will begin to see hyperinflation as a weapon to burn debt, taxes and wages, as in Germany in 1923. One way or another, it seems highly probable that capitalism in the next decade or so is going to spiral *for the first time in its history* into a crisis of *worldwide hyper*inflation. Historically, money is becoming increasingly worthless. As mentioned in our introduction, the US dollar lost more than 96%

of its purchasing power between 1913 and the end of 2019. That means today's dollar is worth less than four cents of the 1913 dollar.[332] Another definite limit approaches. The vast amount of that devaluation actually came after 1949, when today's dollar was worth nine cents – having remained nearly unchanged since 1779 – and even more so since 1970. Proponents of the subjective theory of value are obsessed with the comparison to 1913, since that is when the US central bank was founded and the gold standard first suspended. But interest rates have been trending downwards since the fifteenth century. Paul Schmelzing, an economic historian from Harvard University, has produced the most comprehensive survey to date of long-term interest rates:

> The century-average safe real rate peaked in the 15th century at 9.1%, and declined to 6.1% in the 16th century, followed by 4.6% in the 17th, 3.5% in the 18th century, and 1.3% (thus far) for the 21st century…[The overall trend has] persisted across a variety of monetary regimes: fiat- and non-fiat, with and without the existence of public monetary institutions… The long-term historical data suggests that, whatever the ultimate driver, or combination of drivers, the forces responsible have been indifferent to monetary or political regimes; they have kept exercising their pull on interest rate levels irrespective of the existence of central banks, (de jure) usury laws, or permanently higher public expenditures. They persisted in what amounted to early modern patrician plutocracies, as well as in modern democratic environments, in periods of low-level feudal Condottieri battles, and in those of professional, mechanised mass warfare.[333]

It is since the US became the world's foremost capitalist superpower, in its declining imperialist phase, that dollar devaluation has really taken off. Britain, the world's oldest imperialist power, has seen pound sterling devalue by more than 99.5% since it was adopted as the Royal Chartered Bank of England's currency in 1694 (again, mostly since 1970).

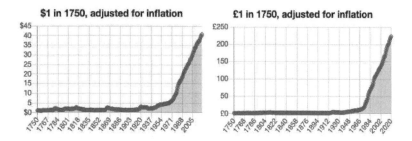

Source: Officialdata.org

Russia and China, among others, started diversifying their foreign currency reserves in the past few years, meaning the main source for paying off US debt is disappearing. In the first quarter of 2020, the US dollar's share of trade between Russia and China fell below 50% for the first time on record, having been as high as 90% in 2015. At the same time, the euro made up an all-time high of 30%, while their national currencies accounted for 24%, also a new high. Even the biggest US bank, JP Morgan, told its clients in August 2019 'it would not be prudent' to invest in the dollar.

While smaller economies have survived defaults through bailouts in the past, the US and western European countries are the richest and most developed in the world. To a significant extent they live off profit produced by labour in Africa, Asia and Latin America.[334] If the imperialist economies collapse, it's because the whole system has collapsed.

If all these converging factors – historically near-zero prices, global deindustrialisation, flat productivity growth, an 'everything bubble' of unsustainably high debt, negative interest rates, exhausted currencies – do not constitute a final breakdown of capitalism, then what will?

Can the IMF bail out all the world's central banks, or even

just the Fed? It seems unlikely, but even if it could, who would then bail out the IMF when the next, even greater breakdown strikes in, say, another decade? Will the price of gold stabilise, enabling it to become a global currency? Perhaps, but again only for a time. Gold production too is being automated. Gold *is* the money-commodity, so if fiat currency collapses then surely so does the monetary status of gold. Anybody without much gold – the vast majority of people – will become increasingly poor and radicalised.

China's interest rate stood at 4.5% before the crash, so 'the workshop of the world' might have just enough room for manoeuvre to last a while longer. After its economy contracted in the first quarter of 2020, by 6.8%, for the first time in decades, the base rate was cut to 2.5%. To survive the deepening global crash, though, China would surely require (having already become the biggest investor in Africa and Latin America) total world domination. This could happen at a time when, if hyperinflation does not produce revolutions first, the imperialist powers would probably try to make up for their lost export markets by turning to direct colonialism, to 'extend' their domestic markets. With its export-oriented economy dependent on demand from world trade that is now collapsing, China too would either have to turn to direct colonialism or conclude its apparent 'capitalist road to socialism'.[335]

If direct colonialism does become the order of the day, it will not stop the march towards full automation. Not to mention the fact that it would be met with increasingly immense resistance – and provoke a global conflict. Of course, that could also happen before then (see below).

Economic necessity

However things play out, world socialism is – *for the first time* – becoming an *absolute* economic *necessity*. From slavery and feudalism to capitalism; and fascism, Keynesian social democracy and neoliberalism – all three became necessary in order to meet the demands of accumulation – economic necessity has always prevailed in the end. Eventually accumulation itself demands socialism.

Just as Grossman contended that the socialist movement's commitment to the overthrow of capitalism required theoretical proof of the system's tendency towards breakdown, theoretical proof that socialism is capitalism's necessary replacement is also required. Marx's materialist conception of history – tracing the historical development of the productive forces – makes this clear:

- Since the private sector tends towards monopolisation and increasing dependence on state subsidies (including tax cuts) – trending towards 100% of income and therefore nationalisation – a 'final merger' is the historically logical next step in the development of the productive forces. Since a total monopoly is impossible under capitalism, this can only be done by taking all the means of production under public ownership; i.e. a public monopoly.
- Since private enterprise has become increasingly dependent on long-term central planning (budgets, forecasts, stock coding, etc.), the productive forces logically now require long-term central planning as a whole.[336] The exponential advances in computing power, digital, data and stock coding now make planning much more practical than was possible at any time during the existence of the Soviet Union.
- Since the private sector is losing its ability to employ value-creating (commodity-producing) labour, society – through an all-socialist state and state/socially owned enterprise – must take over responsibility for employment, enabling full formal employment.
- Since exchange-value is only created under capitalism

through the production and sale of commodities, a workforce that is already largely services-based means economic growth can only be revived under an applicable model, whereby for-profit commodity production is replaced by break-even utility production.

- Since fiat currency is dying a natural death, with cash itself having already mostly disappeared, it must be replaced by a digital voucher system, with the 'currency' pegged to labour time (the true measure of value).[337]
- Since the trend towards 'globalisation' – the integration of nation-states into a world system – has been interrupted by capitalism's final breakdown, world socialism is required to make trade truly free, since no exchange of ownership takes place between social enterprises or nations in a socialist political union.
- In the long run, free time will increasingly become the measure of social wealth (alongside use-values), revitalising independent craftsmanship and experimentation. As full automation, 3-D-printing,[338] lab-grown food, permaculture farming, etc., become increasingly upscaled, diffuse and 'localised', and manufacturing costs fall to zero, socialism (the lower stage of communism) will bring about abundant material wealth *for all*, and the state and class will therefore become increasingly *irrelevant* and *necessarily* wither away – completing the road to (the higher stage of) communism. In this way, *whereas capitalism has a long-term tendency to centralise wealth and power, socialism has a long-term tendency to decentralise wealth and power.*

Just as capitalism matured in the womb of feudalism through the concentration of industry, socialism has matured in the womb of capitalism through the deindustrialisation, servicisation, automation and digitalisation of labour.

Class struggle

We are near and yet so far. The techno-economic base could not be much riper, but the superstructure's resistance is becoming increasingly oppressive and reactionary. Class consciousness – consciousness of the necessity of socialism and the working class's historical mission – along with the willingness to fight back, remains low in most countries, scrambled by the bewildering array of fear-mongering misinformation from the capitalist and reformist mass media. The situation, it seems, is not all that different to what Grossman experienced when he lamented the lack of revolutionary fervour in Germany. His lessons from that period surely indicate that the 'united front from above' tactic has to be applied as consistently and patiently as possible.

History really is made in circumstances we would not choose. It seems that a final, insurmountable breakdown – a historical limit to accumulation – is what it will take to end capitalism. This will increasingly *compel* the *masses* to organise independently of and in militant opposition to the ruling class. The objective conditions for a global revolution will surely become much greater than in the previous century: the world population's share of proletarians is much, much larger; and the private ownership of production is becoming impossible. Opportunism will become 'scarcer and scarcer', as Grossman says. Capital must eventually brutalise and betray one too many people. Inspiration can already be drawn from recent mass struggles in the US, France, India, Bolivia and Haiti, to name a few.

While Grossman agreed with Lenin that no crisis could be considered the final one before it had been cemented by revolution – that there were 'no absolutely hopeless situations' for the capitalists[339] – if Marx was right to regard capitalism's succession by socialism as 'inevitable'[340] and a 'process of natural history', then a final crisis by definition there must be; just as the world revolution must begin with socialism in one country by definition. As Grossman stressed, though, the final capitalists will cling to power until the masses have seized it from them.

Revolutionary parties will have to support and lead the coming struggles in order to help break workers' illusions in *de facto* social democracy. They will need a political programme that makes socialism the most attractive option for the great majority of a given population – the cancellation of *all* personal debt and mortgages,[341] and so on – including incentives to divide the enemy and encourage mass defections, such as amnesty and compensation for expropriations. Socialists need to put sectarianism over single issues that are impossible to resolve aside by committing to a system of participative and direct democracy – so that the masses decide such issues – starting with the promise of a new constitution, written and approved by the people, in each country.

Grossman was right

Against the socialist movement's neglect – and occasional slander – Grossman stands vindicated. If capitalism simply evolved into socialism, as claimed by the likes of Bernstein, then politics would not have taken the deeply reactionary turn we are now experiencing. The succession of worsening global recessions and the trend towards zero in terms of profit and GDP growth rates, prices, currency values and interest rates also show that it is capitalism's tendency towards breakdown, not the Comintern's eclectic disproportionality and underconsumption theory, that explains the final crisis.

Socialist revolutions have succeeded before without a perfect grasp of Marxist economics, but today's burgeoning movement would help itself immensely if it did not make the same mistake. It is not too late to put Grossman alongside Marx at the heart of scientific socialism – doing so would ensure that Marx really is at its heart.

Socialism or extinction?

While the reactionary turn sinks deeper into a new barbarism that threatens to eclipse the atrocities of the twentieth century, humanity now also faces extinction on at least two fronts. The rapidly worsening climate crisis is undoubtedly a manifestation of the demands of capital accumulation. To fend off the breakdown tendency, capitalism has to expand the production of commodities, necessitating more and more extraction, deforestation, intensive agriculture, etc., releasing increasing amounts of previously sequestered carbon dioxide into the atmosphere and warming the planet. The vitality of Grossman's theory, in explaining new developments, or intensifications of existing trends, is clear.

The production process is a labour process and a valorisation process. Because valorisation depends on ever-greater labour exploitation, the labour-intensity of extraction, etc., becomes increasingly necessary. Although these practices are usually now highly mechanised – resulting in their increasing unprofitability – the rate of exploitation of the remaining workers is very high.

Just as surplus value is converted into capital quicker than it is produced, *nature is converted into commodity capital quicker than it can be replenished*. It is not capitalism's 'need for infinite growth on a planet of finite resources', as most leftists seem to put it, that gives rise to the *immediate, central* problem. Rather, it is the *pace* of expansion, determined by the ever-larger *size* of the total functioning capital and its need to expand still further, *relative* to the speed of nature's replenishment – which we hinder under capitalism but could help under socialism – combined with the need to create value based on labour exploitation; for the more non-renewable a material is, the more labour exploitation is involved in its reproduction.

Capitalism has now become a *de facto* extinction cult that can only keep steering the planet into the sun. Socialism gives humanity at least some chance of pulling up to safety in the nick of time. Because socialism produces value through utility production, rather than exploitation, it is not absolutely dependent on extraction, since all work becomes productive. Socialism would therefore be capable of making a transition to non-extractive production through, for example, an industrial revolution that is actually green (unlike the Green New Deal supported by social democrats),[342] i.e. based on hemp and other fibrous plants.[343] Economic output could still increase, fulfilling the communist promise of abundance for all – without which there can be no classless society – but based on: break-even planning *at the rate* nature replenishes, or slower; and renewable (plants, which regrow) rather than non-renewable materials (metals or fossil fuels, which are finite or disappear into thin air).

In his 2019 lecture 'How to enjoy the end of the world', Sid Smith argues convincingly that doubling the size of the economy, as tends to happen every 20 years under capitalism, would finish off Earth's atmosphere – but also that the economy is now so large that the cost of doubling it, based on the expense of a diminishing energy return on investment (EROI), makes that impossible. 'The collapse has already begun,' he says. That this is happening at exactly the same time that capitalism is exhausting its primary fuel supply, *human labour,* can be no coincidence, but it is remarkably humbling nonetheless. Smith's belief that we will return to permanent scarcity is mistaken, however, for his calculations are based on capitalist production. Alongside a plant-based industrial revolution, socialism will also make it possible to re-embrace (emissions-free, energy-dense) nuclear power, which is now safe and clean to produce and use for the large-scale infrastructure that makes energy consumption cheap for the masses – but unprofitable for capital due to the limited amount of labour exploitation and huge upfront costs involved.[344] There is also the prospect of space-based solar power (SBSP) and the associated development of long-range wireless power transmission (also presently too expensive). The available solar energy is ten times that accessed on Earth, without the intermittency of night time or winter. Achieving abundant material wealth for all is *part of the solution* to the climate and environmental crises. Having said that, the need to build relatively localised and communised systems of production and consumption, at least while we are fighting to overcome the new scarcity and limiting emissions while transitioning to nuclear, solar and hemp, is clear and urgent.[345]

The emergence of 3-D-printing and cellular agriculture, making the decentralisation of wealth and power much more possible than in the past, should smooth the way to resocialising the land somewhat and therefore the scaling up of restorative projects and industries, such as reforestation and rewilding. Moving production underground, as the means of production continue to shrink, will create more room for the regeneration of the environment.

Meanwhile, however, the accumulation crisis is also intensifying competition between nation-states over profit, trade, resources and assets, as seen by the rising trade wars and aggressive US posturing towards Iran, China, Russia and even the EU. In 2015-16 – before the Brexit referendum or the election of Trump – the G20 economies introduced a record number of trade-restrictive measures.[346]

In the twentieth century, the destruction of surplus capital and labour brought about by two world wars and fascism – WWI destroyed 35% of the world's total wealth,[347] and yet this was not enough to prevent the Great Depression and WWII – spurred a productivity mega-boom that ended the depression and took imperialism to new heights. Given that the level of overaccumulation is now *much* higher, it follows that a Third World War would have to be *far more* destructive in not just absolute but relative terms. Sternberg's concerns seem more valid in the modern age. Depressions have usually been followed by major wars that have descended into total war.

Given the nuclear threat, a world war would likely finish off the habitability of the atmosphere.

As we saw in chapter three, the masses, as a whole, generally did not begin to fight back in the past, even for relatively modest reforms, until after world wars, to which they had been conscripted, and as mass death turned loose labour markets (high unemployment) into tight ones.[348] The worst hyperinflation ever seen may strike before a world war this time (and the pandemic is producing war-time levels of government spending); while the nuclear threat may breed greater resistance before or during such a war. Can a Leninist commitment to peace galvanise mass defections and revolutions *in* the imperialist and nuclear-holding nations *before* a world war this time, given the nuclear threat? Or at least before the two hands on the Doomsday Clock strike 12?[349]

The 'post-industrial' US – run ragged by wars in Vietnam, Iraq and Afghanistan – has no chance of defeating modern China, now a superpower which has four times the population. Additionally, the arms race would only accelerate the development of automation – and with it capital's final devaluation. Either way, *even a world war surely cannot save capitalism this time*. Socialism or extinction is the choice facing humanity.

* * *

Stead once managed to get Grossman to express why he had dedicated himself to the cause. 'I feel as if I saw a dangerous badly made deadly machine running down the street,' he said in his broken English. 'When it gets to that corner it is going to explode and kill everyone and I must stop it. Once you feel this it gives you great strength. You have no idea, there is no limit to the strength it gives you.'[350]

We must all now find this same great strength.

Endnotes

Introduction

1. Edited by Tony Kennedy for Pluto Press. A full and critical English edition is being prepared by Rick Kuhn, but had not been published at the time of writing.

2. The International Labour Organization (ILO) said 1.6 billion workers in the informal (unregulated) economy alone, nearly half of the world's total workforce, 'stand in immediate danger of having their livelihoods destroyed... The first month of the crisis is estimated to have resulted in a drop of 60% in the income of informal workers globally. This translates into a drop of 81% in Africa and the Americas.' 'ILO: As job losses escalate, nearly half of global workforce at risk of losing livelihoods', ILO [online], 29 April 2020.

3. 'Capital outflows from EMs at record levels in 1Q20, but starting to slow', IntelliNews [online], 9 April 2020.

4. Summers, G., (2017), *The Everything Bubble: The Endgame for Central Bank Policy*, p. 137.

5. Ibid, p. 203.

6. Ibid, p. 143.

7. Average since 1958. The highest was 10.5% in 1981-3; the lowest 3.5% in 1957-8. Ibid, p. 165.

8. See Schmelzing, P., (2020), 'Eight centuries of global real interest rates, R-G, and the "suprasecular" decline, 1311–2018', Bank of England [online].

9. Summers, *op cit*, p. 143.

10. Central banks target a 2% inflation rate since this is low enough to enable businesses to plan around consistent enough prices, but high enough to inspire confidence among spenders and lenders, since deflation is an indicator of recession. (Inflation always amounts to a devaluation of currency, though.) During lockdown, inflation fell to

0.2% in Britain. In the US, the velocity of the M2 money stock (which measures the frequency at which one unit of currency is used to purchase domestically-produced goods and services) fell to a record low of 1.102 for the second quarter (Q2) of 2020, down from 1.427 in Q4 2019 and the highpoint of 2.198 in Q3 1997.

11. Bank of America estimated a BoE rate cut to just minus 0.25% would take 50% off Barclays' domestic pre-tax profit, rising to more than 70% for RBS and Virgin Money.

12. With bailouts, funds come from external sources (another firm, central bank, country, etc.); with bail-ins, funds come from the troubled entity itself.

13. That is, central banks and other major financial institutions maintain large quantities of the US dollar to use for investments, transactions and international debt obligations, or to influence their domestic exchange rate. This gives the US its political power: if two countries want to make a trade, say for oil, they will usually need to make the monetary transaction via a US company. If one of those countries is defying the political wishes of the US, the US can fine any company that enables the transaction, deterring that company's co-operation and thereby undermining that country's ability to trade.

14. 'BoE is financing UK's coronavirus measures, Bailey acknowledges', *Financial Times* [online], 14 May 2020.

15. 'The ballooning money supply may be the key to unlocking inflation in the US', CNBC [online], 5 August 2020.

16. 'What impact does inflation have on the dollar value today?', Investopedia [online], 25 June 2019.

17. Officialdata [online].

18. 'The average life expectancy for a fiat currency is 27 years...Every 30 to 40 years the reigning monetary system fails and has to be retooled', Washington's Blog, 2 August 2011. Pound sterling has lost about 50% of its value against

the US dollar since 1970. Since Britain voted to leave the European Union, pound sterling has evolved 'into a currency that resembles the underlying reality of the British economy: small and shrinking with a growing dual deficit problem similar to more liquid [emerging market] currencies', according to the Bank of America.

19. 'Why coronavirus could spark a capitalist supernova', MR Online, 4 April 2020.

20. Esteban Ezequiel Maito, *The Historical Transience of Capital: The Downward Trend in The Rate of Profit Since XIX Century*, Universidad de Buenos Aires, 2014, p. 18.

21. Grossman, H., *The Law of Accumulation and Breakdown of the Capitalist System* (Abridged), Pluto Press, London, 1992, p. 187.

Chapter 1

22. Letter from Christina Stead to Bill Blake, 10 April 1944. Quoted in Kuhn, R., *Henryk Grossman and the Recovery of Marxism*, University of Illinois Press, 2007, p. 4.

23. Kuhn, *op cit*, p. 1.

24. Ibid, p. 9.

25. Ibid.

26. Ibid, p. 8.

27. Ibid, p. 4.

28. The Second International was founded in 1889. It collapsed in 1914 when most of the various sections of the international supported 'their own' imperialist governments in World War I. In the years between 1889 and 1914, virtually all Marxists as well as many reformists and Labour Party liberals were members of the Second International.

29. Kuhn, *op cit*, p. 8.

30. Ibid, p. 9.

31. Ibid, p. 11.

32. Ibid.

33. Ibid, p. 13.

34. Quoted in ibid.

35. Ibid.

36. Lenin, V.I., 'The National Question in Our Programme', 1903, *Collected Works*, vol. 6, 4th ed., Moscow, Progress Publishers, 1977 [1903], pp. 452-61.

37. Kuhn, *op cit*, p. 14.

38. Quoted in ibid, p. 15.

39. Quoted in ibid, p. 26.

40. Ibid, pp. 16-17.

41. Ibid, p. 24.

42. Ibid.

43. Lenin, 'Does the Jewish Proletariat Need an "Independent Political Party"', *op cit* [1903], p. 332.

44. Kuhn, *op cit*, p. 23.

45. Ibid, p. 35.

46. Quoted in ibid, p. 36.

47. Ibid, p. 40.

48. Ibid, p. 45.

49. Workers' councils ('soviets' in Russian) were institutions of radical democracy that organised production, collectively forming a *de facto* alternate state, creating a situation of dual power with the ruling state. While they were defeated in 1905, they seized power in Russia in 1917. When the bourgeois provisional government, including left-wing reformists, refused the soviets' demands to pull Russia out of WWI, the Bolsheviks grew rapidly and began to win majorities in soviets in a number of major cities. In November 1917 (October according to the old Russian calendar), they achieved a majority in the Second All-Russian Congress of Soviets. The (almost unopposed) insurrection they then organised gave full political authority to the new socialist soviet state.

50. Kuhn, *op cit*, p. 47.

51. Ibid, p. 48.
52. Ibid, p. 47.
53. Ibid, p. 48.
54. Quoted in ibid, p. 50.
55. Ibid, p. 52.
56. Ibid, p. 56.
57. Ibid, p. 64.
58. Ibid, p. 65.
59. Ibid, p. 65-6.
60. Ibid, p. 66.
61. Ibid, p. 77.
62. Ibid, p. 79.
63. Quoted in ibid, p. 82.
64. Ibid, p. 89.
65. Ibid, p. 86.
66. Ibid, p. 112.
67. Ibid, p. 91.
68. Quoted in ibid, p. 92.
69. Ibid, p. 96.
70. Grossman, *Henryk Grossman Works Volume 1, Essays and Letters on Economic Theory*, edited by Kuhn, R., Brill, Leiden, 2019, pp. 44-49.
71. That Marx then works his way back towards empirical reality is discussed in chapter two.
72. Kuhn, *op cit*, p. 97.
73. Ibid, p. 102. The other two were Stefan Rudniański and Adam Ettinger.
74. Ibid, p. 98.
75. (Stead) Ibid.
76. Quoted in ibid, p. 99.
77. Ibid, p. 106.
78. Kuhn, *op cit*, p. 100.
79. Kuhn, *op cit*, p. 103-4.
80. Grossman, 2019, pp. 66-119.

81. Kuhn, *op cit*, p. 108.
82. Ibid.
83. Ibid, p. 114.
84. Quoted in ibid, p. 120.
85. Ibid.
86. Ibid, p. 124.

Chapter 2

87. Reid, A., 'Wall St. lays an egg: the wall street crash, as viewed through the papers', Historic Newspapers [online].
88. Grossman, 1992, p. 197-8.
89. Ibid, p. 33.
90. Ibid, p. 29.
91. Ibid.
92. Ibid, p. 32.
93. Ibid. p. 59.
94. Ibid, p. 33.
95. Lanchester, J., 'The Robots are Coming', *London Review of Books* [online], 5 March 2015.
96. 'The wage worker has permission to work for his own subsistence – that is, to live, only insofar as he works for a certain time *gratis* [free] for the capitalist...that the whole capitalist system of production turns on the increase of this *gratis* labour...consequently, the system of wage labour is a system of slavery, and indeed of a slavery which becomes more severe in proportion as the social productive forces of labour develop, whether the worker receives better or worse payment.' Marx, *Critique of the Gotha Programme*, Dodo Press, 2009 [1875] pp. 18-19.
97. Marx, K., *Capital* Vol I, Penguin Classics, London, 1990, p. 125.
98. Grossman, 1992, p. 155.
99. Ibid, p. 31-2.
100. Ibid, p. 44.

101. The organic composition of capital measures the difference between the rate of surplus value (s/v) and the rate of profit. In general, the higher the organic composition of capital, the more *capital*-intensive the industry, and the lower the rate of profit; the more *labour* intensive, the higher the rate of profit. This tendency has been confirmed by statistical mechanics: see Paul Cockshott (2008), 'How physics is validating the labor theory of value', University of Glasgow.

102. Grossman, 1992, p. 85.

103. Ibid, p. 133.

104. Marx, 1991, p. 358.

105. At least before 1910, after which Kautsky rejected breakdown theory and revolution.

106. Quoted in Grossman, 2019, p. 321.

107. Lenin agreed with some of Hilferding's observations: 'Production becomes social, but appropriation remains private.' Lenin, *Imperialism: The Highest Stage of Capitalism*, Foreign Languages Publishing House, Moscow, 1951 [1916], p. 37.

108. Quoted in Grossman, 2019, p. 354.

109. Bernstein led the campaign to transform the German SPD into an openly reformist, non-revolutionary party. Much later, after WWII, the leaders of the Chinese Communist Party (CCP) claimed that the Communist Party of the Soviet Union (CPSU) under the leadership of Nikita Khrushchev had replaced Leninism with a revisionism analogous to the thought of Bernstein. The CCP later claimed that Khrushchev and his successors had fully restored capitalism in the Soviet Union and even compared them to Nazis. The use of the term 'revisionist' to describe the policies of the CPSU was quietly dropped after Deng Xiaoping became the *de facto* leader of the CCP in 1978 and began a process of opening the Chinese economy up to

foreign investment.

110. Quoted in Kuhn, *op cit*, p. 124.
111. Quoted in Grossman, 1992, p. 39.
112. Quoted in ibid, p. 40.
113. Ibid, p. 45.
114. Ibid, p. 54.
115. Quoted in ibid, p. 55.
116. Ibid, pp. 199-200. Hence why the banks proved to be the weakest link in the chain of capital in the 2007-09 crash – they were compelled to speculate to centralise capital.
117. Ibid.
118. Ibid, p. 126.
119. Ibid, pp. 41-2.
120. Ibid, p. 48.
121. Ibid, pp. 50-51.
122. Ibid, p. 31.
123. Ibid, pp. 67-8.
124. Ibid, p. 71.
125. Ibid.
126. Ibid, p. 72.
127. Ibid, p. 74.
128. Ibid.
129. Grossman, *op cit*, pp. 68, 75.
130. Ibid, p. 81.
131. Ibid, p. 76.
132. Ibid.
133. Ibid, p. 77.
134. Grossman, *op cit*, p. 77-8.
135. Ibid, p. 82.
136. Ibid, p. 87.
137. Ibid.
138. Ibid, p. 108.
139. Marx, *Capital* vol III, Penguin Classics, London, 1991, p. 338.

140. Ibid, p. 361.
141. 'Investors bet giant companies will dominate after crisis', New York Times [online], 28 April 2020.
142. Quoted in Coffey, B., 'The four companies that control the 147 companies that own everything', Forbes [online], 26 October 2011.
143. Tepper, J., and Hearn, D., *The Myth of Capitalism: Monopolies and the Death of Competition*, Wiley, New York, 2018, p. 10.
144. Ibid, p. 9. Lenin called imperialism 'moribund capitalism' since it represented a 'transition to a higher system' of production. Lenin (1974 [1916]), 'Imperialism and the split in socialism', *Collected Works* vol. 23, Progress Publishers, Moscow, p. 107. Indeed, the private sector is increasingly dependent on state subsidies. US government spending represented 2% of national GDP in 1913, but the figure has trended upwards, to 43.73% in 2011. Partly this is due to the absolute rising expense of Medicare and pensions amid an ageing population, but the private sector needs the state to take on the bulk of such costs. Corporations also receive direct subsidies and indirect subsidies like tax cuts. The idea that the private sector does all the innovating is also a myth. The private sector 'only finds the courage to invest after the state has made the high-risk, long-term investments that the private sector cannot afford. The state socialises the risks, while rewards are privatised.' Mariana Mazzucato (2018), *The Entrepreneurial State: Debunking Public vs. Private Sector Myths*, Penguin. In fact, large private research and design centres in the US have 'mostly disappeared' (p. 193).
145. Grossman, 1992, p. 140.
146. Marx, 1991, pp. 442-3.
147. Maito, *op cit*, pp. 18-19.
148. 'Britain's biggest export: wealth', *The Economist*, 9 January 2015.

149. Curtis, M., *The New Colonialism: Britain's Scramble for Africa's Energy and Mineral Resources*, War on Want, July 2016. 'While the scale and scope of the UK's involvement in the exploitation of Africa's mineral resources is staggering, so too is the trail of social, environmental and human rights abuses left in its wake.'

150. Whether the likes of Russia, China, Israel and India have become imperialist is beyond the scope of this discussion.

151. As described in John Smith's 'The GDP Illusion' article for Monthly Review Online (1 July, 2012): a garment worker in Bangladesh is 'paid' €1 for making 18 t-shirts in a 10-hour shift. Each T-shirt is sold in Germany for €4.95 by the Swedish retailer Hennes & Mauritz (H&M); H&M pays the Bangladeshi manufacturing firm €1.35 for each T-shirt, 28% of the final sale price; H&M keeps 60 cents in profit per T-shirt; the German state captures 79 cents through VAT at 19%; the net profit goes towards Germany's, not Bangladesh's, GDP.

152. Quoted in Jason Hickel, 'Aid in Reverse: how poor countries develop rich countries', *The Guardian* [online], 14 January 2017.

153. Grossman, 1992, p. 172.

154. France opposed the 2003 invasion of Iraq because it owned a large chunk of the country's oil infrastructure and did not want the competition from rival imperialist powers.

155. One of Lenin's acute observations was his definition of finance capital: 'Hilferding understands finance capital to be bank capital; he does not ask who stands behind this bank capital...Lenin...understands finance capital...as the merging of monopoly capital, primarily industrial capital, with state power and policy, which is a tool of this capital. That is something quite different. That the banks are facilitators of the expansion of capital is clear. But one has to ask whether, for example, the American bankers play the

chief role in America's economic life, deciding the direction of expansionist American policy. Or are they mere organs of the industrial magnates, who have their representatives in the bank administrations?...I affirm the mighty role of finance capital in Lenin's sense...' Grossman, 2019, p. 231.

156. Grossman, 1992, p. 122.

157. Ibid, p. 181.

158. Ibid.

159. Ibid, p. 197.

160. Ibid, p. 157.

161. Ibid, p. 85.

162. Economic Policy Institution.

163. Bureau of Economic Analysis.

164. See Smith, J., (2016), *Imperialism in the Twenty First Century*, Monthly Review Press, New York, 2016, p. 115. 'Between 1980 and 2005 the proportion of waged and salaried workers in total [in the economically active population] in...the developed nations steadily rose, from 83% to 88% (in 2005, around 500 million people), indicating deepening proletarianisation in these countries.'

165. Quoted in Rick Kuhn, 'Economic Crisis and Socialist Revolution: Henryk Grossman's Law of Accumulation, Its First Critics and His Responses', p. 12 [online]. Originally published in Paul Zarembka and Susanne Soederberg (eds) *Neoliberalism in Crisis, Accumulation, and Rosa Luxemburg's Legacy*, Elsevier Jai, Amsterdam, *Research in Political Economy* 21, 2004, pp. 181-221.

166. Ibid, p. 13.

167. Ibid, p. 14.

168. Ibid.

169. Grossman, 2019, p. 210.

170. Ibid, p. 216.

171. Ibid, p. 234.

172. Kuhn, 2007, p. 140.

173. Grossman, 2019, p. 241.

Chapter 3

174. Chris Harman (1985 [1982]), *The Lost Revolution: Germany 1918 to 1923*, Bookmarks, London Second Ed., p. 47.
175. Ibid, p. 48.
176. Ibid, p. 52.
177. Ibid, pp. 58-9.
178. Ibid, p. 62.
179. Ibid, p. 65.
180. Ibid, p. 69-70.
181. Ibid, p. 71.
182. Ibid, p. 80.
183. Ibid, pp. 77-86.
184. Ibid, pp. 99-100.
185. Ibid, p. 99.
186. Ibid, pp. 145-6.
187. Ibid, p. 187.
188. Ibid, p. 212.
189. Ibid, pp. 199-202.
190. Ibid, p. 215.
191. Ibid, p. 216.
192. Ibid, p. 216.
193. Ibid, p. 225.
194. Ibid, p. 274.
195. Ibid, pp. 274-5.
196. Ibid, p. 275.
197. Ibid, p. 281-2.
198. Ibid, p. 284.
199. Ibid, p. 288.
200. Ibid, p. 289.
201. Ibid, pp. 289-91.
202. Ibid, p. 293.
203. Ibid, p. 295.

204. Ibid, p. 258.

205. Trotsky: 'A party which carries on a protracted revolutionary agitation and then, after the confidence of the masses has raised it to the top, begins to vacillate... paralyses the activity of the masses, sows disillusion and disintegration...and brings ruin to the revolution; but in turn it provides itself with a ready excuse – after the debacle – that the masses were insufficiently active.' Quoted in Harman, pp. 299-300.

206. Lenin had proven more tactically astute than both Stalin and Trotsky during the revolution when he intervened from exile to combat Trotsky's dismissal of the revolutionary potential of the poor peasants – the most important class given that they vastly outnumbered the workers – and Stalin's critical (if temporary) support of the bourgeois provisional government, which had replaced the Tsar, based on the idea that the soviets could pressure the new regime to end the war. (Both came round to Lenin's position.) Lenin opposed premature calls to overthrow the new government, given most soldiers hoped Stalin's proposal would work, but raised the slogan 'no faith in and no support for the Provisional Government'. When the regime broke its promise to end the war it also broke the illusions of the masses – and the soviets swung behind the Bolsheviks. See Patrick Newman, 'April: Lenin re-arms Bolshevik vanguard: Russia 1917 part 3', revolutionatycommunist.org, 4 April 2017 [*Fight Racism, Fight Imperialism* 68, May 1987].

207. Abraham, D., (1986), *The Collapse of the Weimar Republic: Political Economy and Crisis*, Second Edition, Holmes & Meier, New York, p. 280.

208. Abraham, *op cit*, p. 260.

209. Ibid, pp. 304-14.

210. Ibid, p. 283.

211. Ibid, p. 269.
212. Ibid, p. 286.
213. Ibid, pp. 317-18.
214. See 'Germà Bel (2006), Against the Mainstream: Nazi Privatization in 1930s Germany', University of Barcelona.
215. Grossman, 2019, p. 245.
216. 2.6% in 1928; 18.3% in 1930; 37.3% in 1932.
217. Grossman, 2019, pp. 233-4.
218. Harman, *op cit*, p. 305.
219. Abraham, *op cit*, p. 313.
220. Harman, *op cit*, p. 305.
221. Ibid, p. 307.
222. Stalin, J., 'Concerning the International Situation', 20 September 1924, Marxist Internet Archive [online].
223. K, J., 'Fighting Fascism: Communist Resistance to the Nazis, 1928-1933', Cosmonaut.blog, July 2019.
224. K, *op cit*.
225. Ibid.
226. Grossman, 2019, p. 239.
227. Ibid, p. 242.
228. Trotsky, 'The German Catastrophe: The responsibility of the leadership', May 1933, marxists.org. 'Instead of helping to aggravate the discord between Communism's principal political adversary and its mortal foe – for which it would have been sufficient to proclaim the truth aloud instead of violating it – the Communist International convinced the reformists and the fascists that they were twins; it predicted their conciliation, embittered and repulsed the social democratic workers, and consolidated their reformist leaders.'
229. Grossman, 2019, p. 247.
230. Grossman, 2019, p. 254.
231. Ibid, p. 260.
232. Grossman, 2019, pp. 261-2.

233. Ibid, p. 264.

234. Kuhn, 2007, p. 145.

235. Kuhn, *op cit*, p. 162.

236. Quoted in Kuhn, *op cit*, p. 169.

237. Ibid, p. 171.

238. 'The Programme of the Communist International. Comintern Sixth Congress 1928', Marxist Internet Archive [online].

239. Quoted in Kuhn, *op cit*, p. 174.

240. Grossman, 2019, p. 422.

241. Quoted in Kuhn, *op cit*, p. 175.

242. Grossman, 2019, p. 255-6.

243. Ibid, p. 258.

244. Ibid, p. 240.

245. In *Critique of the Gotha Programme* Marx explains that socialism will replace money with non-transferable vouchers pegged to labour time. Such a move (even if money was used only as an index) was surely made impossible by the Soviet Union's underdevelopment and need to trade with capitalist countries (whose unpredictable, fluctuating prices also undermined its ability to plan and encouraged the allowance of a black market to bring in foreign currency, upon which it eventually become too dependent. It also has to be remembered that the arms race forced by the US came at the expense of the civilian economy.) While this strengthens the argument that socialism has to become global to survive, with money now having been all but completely digitised it would arguably now be possible to have a digital voucher system even in one (albeit powerful) country. For a critique of Soviet economics, see Cockshott, P. and Cottrell, A. (1993), *Towards A New Socialism,* Spokesman, Nottingham.

246. Grossman, 2019, pp. 263-4.

247. Marx, 2009, p. 8.

248. Marx, 2009, p. 8.
249. Kuhn, 2007, p. 170; Jean, 2007.
250. Ibid, p. 184.
251. Ibid, p. 157.
252. Ibid.
253. Quoted in ibid, p. 158.
254. Grossman, 2019, pp. 455-8. Although the absolute growth in slaves in the US continued to grow, the number relative to the whole population tended to fall before slavery was abolished in the US (approx. 25% in 1790 versus 16% in 1860). Similarly, the proportion of manufacturing workers in the US workforce has tended to fall as capitalism ages (40% in 1945; 26.4% in 1970; 8.7% in 2015).
255. Ibid, p. 411.
256. Grossman, 'The Beginnings of Capitalism and the New Mass Morality', 1934, Marxist Internet Archive [online].
257. Grossman, 2019, p. 411.
258. Freudenthal, G. (2005), 'The Hessen-Grossman Thesis: An Attempt at Rehabilitation', Perspectives on Science, vol. 13, no. 2, p. 172.
259. Ibid, p. 175.
260. Grossman, 1934.
261. Religion is dying alongside the law of value, at least in the most economically advanced countries – 70% of 16- to 29-year-olds in Britain identify with no religion, for example, according to a study by St Mary's University. Marx wrote that 'the miracles of gods [are] rendered superfluous by the miracles of industry...' Economic and Philosophic Manuscripts of 1844 (2011), Wilder Publications, Blacksburg (US), p. 50. Rising scarcity as capitalism collapses is likely to see religion rise again somewhat. Religion and all superstition will begin to wither away again under socialism and more or less disappear once fully automated production brings about abundant

material wealth for all.

262. Freudenthal, *op cit*, p. 174.
263. In 1934, Grossman told Beer that 'I give the first – so far as I know – outline of a materialist history of mechanics from the 14th century to Descartes.' In fact, a Russian Marxist, Boris Hessen, had made an important contribution in this area in 1931 on the social and economic roots of Newton's Principia. By 1937, Grossman was aware of Hessen's study and regarded it as complementary to his own work. Kuhn, *op cit*, p. 165.
264. This was especially true of 'Materialism and Metaphysics' and 'On Bergson's Metaphysics of Time'.
265. Grossman, 2019, p. 433.
266. Ibid. See Horkheimer, M., 2002 [1937], 'The Latest Attack on Metaphysics', in *Max Horkheimer, Critical Theory: Selected Essays*, New York: Continuum, pp. 132-87.
267. Ibid, p. 19.
268. Kuhn, 2007, p. 187.
269. Ibid, p. 192.
270. Quoted in ibid, p. 192.
271. Ibid, p. 195.
272. Quoted in Ibid, p. 199.
273. Grossman, 2019, p. 625.
274. Quoted in Kuhn, *op cit*, pp. 198-204.
275. Ibid, p. 201.
276. Ibid, p. 209.
277. Ibid, p. 222.
278. Ibid, p. 214.
279. Ibid, p. 215.
280. Ibid, p. 216.
281. Ibid, p. 218.
282. Ibid, p. 222. Grossman's work did not gain attention again until the late 1960s. It was initially rediscovered by activists in West Germany. In the Anglosphere, Mattick expounded

Grossman's crisis theory in the 1930s and brought it to a wider audience in the 1960s. See *Marx and Keynes* (London, Merlin, 1974 [1969]); and *Economic Crisis and Crisis Theory* (London, Merlin, 1981 [1974]). It was further cited by: David Yaffe, 'The Marxian Theory of Crisis, Capital and the State', (*Economy and Society* 2 (1973), pp. 186-232); Anwar Shaikh, 'An Introduction to the History of Crisis Theories', *US Capitalism in Crisis* (New York, Union for Radical Political Economics, 1978, pp. 219-41); and Chris Harman, *Explaining the Crisis* (London, Bookmarks, 1984).

283. Ibid, p. 220.

Chapter 4

284. Grossman, 2019, pp. 120-76.

285. Grossman emphasised 'cannot'.

286. Grossman's emphasis.

287. Grossman, 2019, pp. 304-31.

288. Quoted in Kuhn, R., 'Introduction to Henryk Grossman "The value-price transformation in Marx and the problem of crisis"', *Historical Materialism* issue 1, vol. 24, Brill, p. 98.

289. Grossman, 2019, pp. 332-88.

290. Given the bulk of workers followed the reformists ahead of the revolutionaries in most countries, including initially in Russia – even after being sent by reformists to the slaughterhouse of WWI; *and* after Germany had lost its empire – Lenin's other argument that 'trade union consciousness' (see *What Is To Be Done?*) is the default mode of consciousness of the working class – i.e. without the intervening influence of revolutionaries during a revolutionary situation – is perhaps the most compelling of the three arguments, given that reformists have also been more popular in non-imperialist nations where 'the left' is strong (such as Venezuela, Bolivia and India).

291. Grossman, 2019, pp. 446-49.

292. Lenin, 1951, p. 104.
293. Mechanisation had already had a profound impact on US farming by 1900: the labour needed to produce 1 acre of wheat fell from 61 hours in 1830 to 3 hours 19 minutes in 1896. Reynolds, B., *The Coming Revolution: Capitalism in the 21st Century*, Zer0 Books, *op cit*, loc 1757. Today, the agriculture problem is returning to the bleak days of the Great Depression, when the US government bought produce for a guaranteed profit or ordered its destruction to raise prices. From 1996 to 2006, the cost of producing corn was higher than its sale price. Rising demand as a result of droughts, crop failures and biofuel production boosted prices for a while, but corn production became unprofitable again by 2015. This 'demonstrates that Marx's remarkable prediction was right. The collapse of production for exchange-value is not just a theoretical possibility. We can already observe it happening. An agricultural system that sacrificed everything from environmental standards to food quality and safety in the search for profit can no longer sustain production for profit on an independent basis. US agriculture has to be subsidised permanently or it will be unable to operate in a capitalist market.' Reynolds, *op cit*, loc 1789-1805.
294. Grossman, 1992, p. 183.
295. In 1900 gold was established as the only metal for redeeming paper currency, with the value of gold set at $20.67 an ounce. The US and major European countries suspended the gold standard during WWI so that they could print enough money to fund their military activity. A modified gold standard re-established after the war then had to be abandoned to tackle deflation and mass unemployment. In 1933, the US government made it illegal to hoard gold and set the price at $35 per ounce. After WWII most countries pegged their currencies to the dollar, since the US held

most of the world's gold. Central banks maintained fixed exchange rates between their currencies and the dollar by buying their own country's currency in foreign exchange markets if their currency became too low relative to the dollar. If it became too high, they'd print more of their currency and sell it. As the US economy prospered, US Americans bought more imported goods and paid in dollars. This large balance of payments deficit (money owed to other countries) made foreign governments worry that the US would no longer back up the dollar in gold. In the 1970s, double-digit inflation and stagnant growth reduced the value of the eurodollar [the Soviet Union's dollar reserves deposited in Europe] and more and more banks started redeeming their holdings for gold. The US could no longer meet this growing obligation. The US government changed the dollar-gold relationship to $38 per ounce and no longer allowed the Fed to redeem dollars with gold, which made the gold standard meaningless. Gold was repriced to $42.22 per ounce in 1973 and then decoupled from the dollar altogether in 1976. In 1980 the price of gold had shot up to $600. In August 2020 it jumped to $2000 from $1400 a year earlier. All this shows the prescience of Marx's analysis that prices *increasingly* deviate from their real labour values. 'History of the Gold Standard', The Balance [online], 24 April 2020.

296. Ibid, pp. 469-533.

297. Marx, K., and Engels, F. (1975 [1844]), 'Economic and Philosophic Manuscripts of 1844', *Collected Works* vol. 3, Lawrence & Wishart, p. 316.

298. Grossman, 2019, pp. 556-9.

299. Quoted in Grossman, 2019, p. 433.

Chapter 5

300. 'This was the fastest 30% sell-off ever, exceeding the pace

of declines during the Great Depression', CNBC [online], 23 March 2020.

301. Pento, M., *The Coming Bond Market Collapse*, Wiley, New Jersey, 2013, p. 24.

302. Ibid.

303. Surz, R., 'Per capita world debt has surged to over $200,000', Nasdaq [online], 24 July 2019.

304. 'Global Debt is now 2.5 times the total Money Supply – the system is clearly unworkable', Simon Thorpe Ideas [online], 15 February 2015.

305. Monetary Base, St Louis Federal Reserve [online].

306. M2 Money Stock, St Louis Federal Reserve [online].

307. See '244: Michael Pento: The Coming Bond Market Collapse: How to Survive the Demise of the US Debt', Cashflow Ninja, Youtube video, 27 December 2017.

308. Pento, *op cit*, pp. 141-5.

309. Hart-Landsberg, M., 'Portrait of the 2009-2019 US expansion', Monthly Review Online, 20 June 2019.

310. Quoted in Smith, 'Why coronavirus could spark a capitalist supernova', MR Online, 4 April 2020.

311. Martens P., Martens R., 'The Federal Reserve now owns 15 percent of the US Treasury Market; at its current rate, it could own the whole market in less than two years', Wall Street on Parade [online], 28 March 2020.

312. 'Michael Pento – This is a Global Depression', USA Watchdog [online], 1 April 2020.

313. Aaron Bastani (2019), *Fully Automated Luxury Communism*, Verso, p. 123.

314. Quoted in Stewart, H., 'Robot revolution: rise of "thinking" machines could exacerbate inequality', The Guardian [online], 5 November 2015.

315. Norton, A., 'Automation will end the dream of rapid economic growth for poorer countries', The Guardian [online], 20 September 2016.

316. 'Premature deindustrialization in the developing world', Dan Rodrik's Weblog [online], 12 February 2015.

317. Monbiot, G., 'Lab-grown food will soon destroy farming – and save the planet', The Guardian [online], 2 January 2020.

318. Quoted in Bastani, *op cit*, p. 146.

319. PA Media, 'Bosses speed up automation as virus keeps workers home', The Guardian [online], 30 April.

320. Ibid.

321. About 30% of remote workers in a UK survey said they were working more unpaid hours than before lockdown, with 18% reporting at least four additional unpaid hours a week. See Allegretti, A., 'Ministers urged to give UK home-workers a "right to disconnect"', The Guardian [online], 13 April 2021.

322. Hinsliff, G., 'The next wave of coronavirus disruption? Automation', The Guardian [online], 30 April 2020.

323. Marx, K., *Grundrisse*, Penguin Classics, London, 1993, pp. 705-6. Originally published in 1858.

324. Kuhn, R., 'Capitalism's Collapse: Henryk Grossman's Marxism', *Science & Society* vol. 59, 1995, p. 176.

325. Grossman, 1992, p. 187.

326. Ibid.

327. Ibid.

328. Marx, *op cit*, p. 360.

329. My calculation. Source: World Bank data: GDP growth (annual %) - High income [online].

330. Despite slowing growth, Sweden's Riksbank raised its target rate to zero in July, due to fears over inflating asset prices, after lowering it to minus 0.10% in 2015 and then minus 0.50% in 2016. Jay Powell, who took over as Fed chair in 2018, said that 'moderate' inflation above 2% may be tolerated on a temporary basis to make up for months of below-normal inflation. The median forecast

of Fed officials does not predict an interest rate increase until after 2022 at the earliest. Powell has previously said that the Fed is 'not thinking about thinking' about raising rates – but also admitted that 'the Fed has less scope to support the economy during an economic downturn by simply cutting the federal funds rate'. When the time comes, however, he may feel there is no other choice but to try. With the risk of pent-up demand meeting depleted supply chains were the lockdown to be fully lifted, a recipe for high inflation, the ruling class may have very little incentive to ever fully lift lockdowns. The ruling class has also taken the opportunity to roll back civil rights. Civics Monitor reported in December 2020 that 87% of the global population now live in nations that are 'closed', 'repressed' or 'obstructed', up by 4% on a year earlier. 'The use of detention as the main tactic to restrict protests only shows the hypocrisy of governments using covid-19 as a pretense to crack down on protests, [as] the virus is more likely to spread in confined spaces like prisons.'

331. Gudmundson, E., 'Secretary geithner sends debt limit letter to Congress', Treasury [online], 1 June 2011.

332. Bureau of Labor Statistics' Consumer Price Index inflation calculator.

333. Schmelzing, *op cit*, p. 40.

334. According to the IMF, the total corporate debt of indigenous non-financial firms in major emerging markets, minus China, snowballed from $4 trillion in 2004 to $23.7 trillion in 2015, 90% of total emerging market GDP. Kynge, J. and Wheatley J., 'Emerging Asia: the ill wind of deflation', *Financial Times* [online], 4 October 2015. China's debt exploded from $7 trillion in 2007 to $35 trillion in 2018. Lui, J., 'Next China: The ticking debt bomb', *Bloomberg* [online] 29 November 2019.

335. Whether taking a 'state capitalist road to socialism' has

truly been the intention of the CPC since its liberalising reforms after 1979 – the party claims the country will be socialist by 2050 – or whether the party has been taken over by pro-capitalist social democrats is beyond the scope of this discussion. (The number of Socially Owned Enterprises in China fell from 262,000 in 1997 to 110,000 by 2008 but rose back up to 173,000 by 2016.) What is beyond dispute is the fact that China has embraced some form of capital investment. This is often defended on the basis that Lenin embraced a 'New Economic Policy', concessions made to capital to overcome suffocating trade blockades in 1921. This, however, ended in 1929, by which time socialist planning had taken over the whole economy. With its increasing debt crisis, China – which has overtaken the US as a trading partner with Africa and Latin America – is now suffering from severe overaccumulation. China's liberalisation was the intended (and arguably inevitable, given its need to trade) manifestation of the US's targeted monopolisation of raw materials in south-east Asia. China's underdevelopment in 1949 was badly behind even early twentieth century Russia (China had been self-sufficient before the Opium Wars inflicted by Britain).

336. Central planning does not imply that all decisions are made by an 'elitist' central committee. It is the logical way of coordinating production, distribution and co-operation between all economic and geographic sectors in a country; just as a town council oversees a number of neighbourhoods or a regional council a number of towns. Much planning can even be automated now.

337. For example, 6.5 hours of work earns you 6.5 credits. Workers receive all the value they create, minus deductions for social expenditure, such as universal health care, etc. Units of labour time will be graded according to the type of work and productivity rates to incentivise types of work

where it is needed. This system institutionalises equality of labour (the right to receive all the value you create, which includes access to the deductions that are now socially instead of privately owned), underpinning equal rights and minimising economic inequality; and consistently raises living standards for all through falling prices. Since digital voucher credits will be non-transferable, cancelled like train tickets once 'spent', the centralisation of wealth into the hands of an aristocratic minority becomes impossible, seriously undermining the imperatives behind crime and corruption. Vouchers will be used to 'purchase' consumer goods from the 'common store' that are priced against the labour time it took to produce them, adjusted according to supply and demand to ensure break-evenness. This system makes budgeting far more intelligible, enabling a more informed electorate. For a detailed explanation, see *Towards a New Socialism*.

338. 3-D printing is a type of additive manufacturing, which is far more flexible than traditional manufacturing, since products are built by layering component materials from the bottom up. While commercial prices of 3-D printers fell from $100,000 in 1988 to $1400 in 2015, open source designs can be assembled for as little as $300. The first printers have only been able to print in plastic or steel, but the development of continuous composite printing means they will be able to work with multiple complementary materials simultaneously. Scientists have even developed the ability to print living human kidneys and artificial skin. Edible products like structures made of chocolate or sugar can also be printed and decent sized housing structures can already be printed for as little as $5000. In the future it is likely that printers will be capable of producing goods at the molecular level, i.e. capable of printing anything composed of the molecules used. Ben Reynolds describes

additive production – which 'fulfils the promise of the personal computer as a means of production' – as a paradigm shift from industrial production to distributive production. 'It is conceivable that the logical fulfilment of distributed production – nearly instant production of anything, at will, anywhere in the world – will arrive within the lifetime of children born at the time of this writing... Distributed production fundamentally erodes the basic pillars of capitalism...Any industry that finds itself competing with a form of distributed production will no longer have the option of adaptation through monopolisation. Instead, that industry will flail wildly as prices fall back toward their values and as its entire business model disintegrates in slow motion.' Reynolds, *op cit*, loc 589-673, 1813.

339. Quoted in Kuhn, 2007, p. 130.
340. Marx and Engels, *The Communist Manifesto*, Penguin Classics, 2015, p. 20.
341. In this way, the privately-owned property of housing will be transformed into personal property, like cars. Taking up the position of expropriating private housing would be an ultraleft position that would drive the downwardly mobile middle classes into the arms of reaction and weaken the chances of securing defections and capitulations. It will also be necessary in some shape or form to compensate those losing out from cancelled debt owed to them, such as pensioners (for example, through a guaranteed, good public pension).
342. The Green New Deal relies on expanded resource and wealth extraction from poor and developing nations, whereby replacing oil, gas and coal involves plundering from the earth the cobalt, lithium, silver, copper, plastic, concrete, steel, etc., needed to build wind turbines, solar panels and supercapacitors through processes that

are fuel-intensive. The Organisation for Economic Co-operation and Development's *Global Resources Outlook* to 2060, modelled on an annual 2.8% global growth in GDP, estimates that extracted resources would increase from 79 billion to 167 billion tonnes, a 111% increase overall, with a 150% increase in metals and a 135% increase in minerals. Resource extraction is responsible for 50% of global emissions, with minerals and metal mining responsible for 20% of emissions even before the manufacturing stage. See Rehman, A., 'The "green new deal" supported by Ocasio-Cortez and Corbyn is just a new form of colonialism', The Independent [online], 4 May 2019.

343. Hemp can be converted into 50,000+ products, including biofuel up to two-thirds cleaner than fossil fuel; biodegradable bioplastic up to ten times stronger than steel, yet lighter than carbon fibre; carbon-negative hempcrete; and batteries and conductors that outperform lithium and graphene – at a fraction of the price. While growing, hemp – which requires little water, making it drought-resistant – reverses desertification and rapidly draws down carbon from the atmosphere. See references. Hemp has been prohibited by monopoly capitalism precisely because its versatility, potential abundance and cheapness – since it grows quickly and its production is not labour intensive – is such a threat to fossil fuel, mining, deforestation and other extractive industries. Similarly to hemp's versatility, mycelium, the fungus mushrooms are made of, can be coaxed, using temperature, CO_2, humidity and airflow, to rapidly build fibrous structures for things such as 'packaging, clothing, food and construction – everything from leather to plant-based steak to scaffolding for growing organs' and computers; all with minimal (mostly compostable) waste and energy consumption. See Bayer, E., 'The mycelium revolution is upon us', Scientific

American [online], 1 July 2019; and Adamatzky, A., 'Towards fungal computer', The Royal Society [online], 19 October 2018.

344. See the chapter on nuclear power in Phillips, L., *Austerity Ecology & the Collapse-porn Addicts: A defence of growth, progress, industry and stuff*, Zero Books, Winchester (UK).

345. Communal forms of living will economise consumption and socialise/share out the burden of domestic work. Clearly this has to be carefully and ambitiously planned to respect individuality and privacy. The transition to communal living should be incentivised by tax cuts and rent reductions.

346. 'WTO warns on rise of protectionist measures by G20 economies', *Financial Times* [online], 21 June 2016.

347. Grossman, 1992, p. 157.

348. Labour militancy has often been most powerful as loose labour markets (high unemployment, which enables employers to easily replace workers, compelling the latter to accept lower wages) turn into tight labour markets (high/full employment, and therefore diminished competition between workers), i.e. following plague, famine, or war, making the demand for labour higher and therefore increasing labour's bargaining position and economic independence as a whole. Such militancy has usually ended in compromise between capital and labour, even after extremely bloody continent- or globe-straddling conflicts. The similarities between labour's massive gains in 'the Golden Age of the European proletariat' of approx. 1350-1500 (the overthrow of serfdom, etc), after the Black Death, versus the following four centuries of rollbacks (enclosure, etc); and the post-WWI/II gains (a number of socialist revolutions plus numerous social democracies that included significant nationalisation programmes) versus the post-1973 rollbacks (globally)

are very striking. Two obvious differences: firstly, labour 'went further' in the second period of gains, presumably because the number of poor peasants and labourers had grown relative to the number of landlords and capitalists; and because the economic crisis was deeper; secondly, the second period of gains and rollbacks took place over a shorter period of time (approx. 150 (gains) versus 400 years in the first; 70 versus 45 and counting in the second), indicating that history tends to accelerate/periods of class struggle tend to shorten, presumably because of technological innovation and, again, the growth of labour relative to capital and the deepening of economic crisis, i.e. the greater level of overaccumulation. The final crisis combined with the automation revolution, however, poses the likely problem of an ever-looser labour market, amid populations exponentially greater than even a century ago. Marx certainly thought developments that 'put the majority of the population out of [work]' would 'cause a revolution' (1991, p. 372). With automation abolishing the source of profit, compromise and reform (likely driven at least partly in the past by general war-weariness rather than simply opportunism or labour aristocracies) *will* not be an option this time.

349. The Doomsday Clock is a symbol that represents the likelihood of a man-made global catastrophe, maintained since 1947 by the Bulletin of the Atomic Scientists. In January 2020 the clock was moved to 100 seconds to midnight, closer to midnight than ever before.

350. Quoted in Kuhn, *op cit*, p. 202.

References

Abraham, D. (1986), *The Collapse of the Weimar Republic: Political Economy and Crisis*, Second Edition, Holmes & Meier, New York.

Adamatzky, A. (2018), 'Towards fungal computer', The Royal Society [online]. Available at: https://royalsocietypublishing. org/doi/10.1098/rsfs.2018.0029 (Accessed 1 March 2021).

Allegretti, A. (2021), 'Ministers urged to give UK home-workers a "right to disconnect"', The Guardian [online]. Available at: https://www.theguardian.com/society/2021/ apr/13/ministers-urged-to-give-uk-home-workers-a-right-to-disconnect (Accessed 13 April 2021).

Amadeo, K. (2020), 'History of the Gold Standard', The Balance [online]. Available at: https://www.thebalance.com/what-is-the-history-of-the-gold-standard-3306136 (Accessed 11 November 2020).

Bastani, A. (2019), *Fully Automated Luxury Communism*, Verso, London.

Bayer, E. (2019), 'The mycelium revolution is upon us', Scientific American [online]. Available at: https://blogs. scientificamerican.com/observations/the-mycelium-revolution-is-upon-us/ (Accessed 1 March 2021).

Bel, G. (2006), *Against the Mainstream: Nazi Privatization in 1930s Germany*, University of Barcelona. Available at: http://dx.doi. org/10.2139/ssrn.895247

Board of Governors of the Federal Reserve System, 'Monetary Base', St Louis Federal Reserve [online]. Available at https://fred.stlouisfed.org/series/BOGMBASE (Accessed 15 November 2020).

Board of Governors of the Federal Reserve System, 'M2 Money Stock' St Louis Federal Reserve [online]. https://fred. stlouisfed.org/series/M2 (Accessed 15 November 2020).

BNE IntelliNews (2020), 'Capital outflows from EMs at record levels in 1Q20, but starting to slow' [online]. Available at https://www.intellinews.com/capital-outflows-from-ems-at-record-levels-in-1q20-but-starting-to-slow-180630/ (Accessed 15 April 2020).

Briggs, J. (2012), 'Hemp fuel guide', Hemp Frontiers. Available at: https://hempfrontiers.com/hemp-fuel-guide/ (Accessed 1 April 2019)

Cashflow Ninja, '244: Michael Pento: The Coming Bond Market Collapse: How to Survive the Demise of the US Debt', Youtube video. Available at https://www.youtube.com/watch?v=wMTrImkSrwQ (Accessed 15 September 2019).

Christensen, N. (2020), 'Global gold demand fell 1% in 2019 despite record investor buying', Kitco [online]. Available at https://www.kitco.com/news/2020-01-30/Global-gold-demand-fell-1-in-2019-despite-record-investor-buying-World-Gold-Council.html (Accessed 3 August 2020).

CNBC, 'This car made from hemp cannabis is stronger than steel', Youtube video. Available at https://www.youtube.com/watch?v=TugMbfnA3GI (Accessed 3 April 2019).

Cockshott. W.P. (2008), *How Physics is Validating the Labour Theory of Value*, University of Glasgow.

Cockshott, W.P.; Cottrell, A. (1993), *Towards a New Socialism,* Spokesman, Nottingham.

Coffey, B. (2011), 'The Four Companies That Control the 147 Companies That Own Everything', Forbes [online]. Available at https://www.forbes.com/sites/brendancoffey/2011/10/26/the-four-companies-that-control-the-147-companies-that-own-everything/?sh=631dfc15685b (Accessed 31 December 2020).

Curtis M. (2016), *The New Colonialism: Britain's Scramble for Africa's Energy and Mineral Resources*, War on Want, London.

de Blas et al. (2020), 'The limits of transport decarbonization under the current growth paradigm', *Energy Strategy Reviews* vol. 32, 100543. Available at: https://doi.org/10.1016/j. esr.2020.100543

de Wit, W. et al. (2020), World Wildlife Fund, *WWF Report: COVID-19: Urgent Call to Protect People and Nature.* Available at https://www.worldwildlife.org/publications/covid19-urgent-call-to-protect-people-and-nature

Donnon, S. (2016), 'WTO warns on rise of protectionist measures by G20 economies', *The Financial Times* [online]. Available at https://www.ft.com/content/2dd0ecc4-3768-11e6-a780-b48ed7b6126f (Accessed 17 July 2018).

Elinor, J., *Politics and Culture* [2009] Available at https://politicsandculture.org/2009/10/02/elinor-jean-%E2%80%98the-innovation-of-henryk-grossman%E2%80%99s-marxism%E2%80%99-a-review-of-rick-kuhn-henryk-grossman-and-the-recovery-of-marxism/ (Accessed 6 September 2020).

Federal Reserve Bank of St Louis, 'Velocity of M2 Money Stock' [online]. Available at https://fred.stlouisfed.org/series/M2V (Accessed: 1 October 2020).

Franck, T. (2020), 'The ballooning money supply may be the key to unlocking inflation in the US', CNBC [online]. Available at https://www.cnbc.com/2020/08/05/the-ballooning-money-supply-may-be-the-key-to-unlocking-inflation-in-the-us. html

Freudenthal, G. (2005), 'The Hessen-Grossman Thesis: An Attempt at Rehabilitation', *Perspectives on Science*, vol. 13, no. 2, pp. 166-93.

Grossman, H. (1934), 'The Beginnings of Capitalism and the New Mass Morality', Marxist Internet Archive. Available at https://www.marxists.org/archive/grossman/1934/beginnings.htm (Accessed 14 August 2020).

Grossman, H. (1992 [1929]), *The Law of Accumulation and Breakdown of the Capitalist System (Being also a Theory of Crisis)* (Abridged), Pluto Press, London.

Grossman, H. (2019), *Henryk Grossman Works vol. I: Essays and Letters on Economic Theory*, edited by Rick Kuhn, Brill, Leiden.

Gudmundson, E. (2011), 'Secretary Geithner Sends Debt Limit Letter to Congress', US Department of the Treasury [online]. Available at https://www.treasury.gov/connect/blog/Pages/letter.aspx (Accessed 1 December 2020).

Harman, C. (1984), *Explaining the Crisis*, Bookmarks, London.

Harman, C. (1985 [1982]), *The Lost Revolution: Germany 1918 to 1923*, Second Ed., Bookmarks, London.

Hart-Landsberg, M. (2019), *Reports from the Economic Front* [online]. Available at https://economicfront.wordpress.com/2019/06/18/portrait-of-the-2009-2019-us-expansion/ (Accessed 30 June 2019).

Hemp.com, 'History of hemp' [online] Available at https://www.hemp.com/history-of-hemp/ Accessed 1 April 2019).

Hickel J. (2017), 'Aid in reverse: how poor countries develop rich countries', The Guardian [online]. Available at https://www.theguardian.com/global-development-professionals-network/2017/jan/14/aid-in-reverse-how-poor-countries-develop-rich-countries (Accessed 8 February 2019).

Hill, G. (2017), 'Hemp, and lots of it, could be one climate solution', Huffington Post [online]. Available at https://www.huffpost.com/entry/hemp-and-lots-of-it-could_b_328275?guccounter=1&guce_referrer=aHR0cHM6Ly93d3cuZ29vZ2xlLmNvbS88&guce_referrer_sig=AQAAANj9atSIGrxd6NPk2BrOEbCp9YB7rTeJ_23_CX66R4yluCKvixYLqvpmkzoWPv5XH-Ue1b1ZuVGCSIWZRjuyajm3nJJC_P610Xz3BVacoRxmX-Vwf7qDB994Qg61N936FW3u2NY1Zfq6CUNP0BhdeuPzFquZ8AMab0WQ12NGAe2S (Accessed 2 April 2019).

Hinsliff, G. (2020), 'The next wave of coronavirus disruption? Automation', The Guardian [online]. Available at https://www.theguardian.com/commentisfree/2020/apr/30/coronavirus-disruption-automation (Accessed 30 April 2020).

International Labour Organization (2020), 'ILO: As job losses escalate, nearly half of global workforce at risk of losing livelihoods', [online]. Available at https://www.ilo.org/global/about-the-ilo/newsroom/news/WCMS_743036/lang--en/index.htm (Accessed 1 May 2020).

Kaucic, G. (2019), 'A sustainable alternative to fossil fuels: hemp & biofuel', Hemp History Week [online]. Available at https://www.hemphistoryweek.com/post/a-sustainable-alternative-to-fossil-fuels-hemp-biofuel?fbclid=IwAR3yRPePfdTOvd3j66U7vj3WvOn6D8oE3YgdNeq7sH9z_wpXHH2HQyb-PZw (Accessed 2 April).

Kynge, J. and Wheatley J. (2015), 'Emerging Asia: the ill wind of deflation', *Financial Times* [online].

K, J. (2019), 'Fighting Fascism: Communist Resistance to the Nazis, 1928-1933', Cosmonaut [blog]. Available at https://cosmonaut.blog/2019/01/07/fighting-fascism-communist-resistance-to-the-nazis-1928-1933/ (Accessed 17 August).

Kuhn, R. (1995), 'Capitalism's Collapse: Henryk Grossman's Marxism', *Science & Society* vol. 59, p. 174-92.

Kuhn, R. (2004), 'Economic Crisis and Socialist Revolution: Henryk Grossman's Law of Accumulation, Its First Critics and His Responses', *Research in Political Economy* 21, Amsterdam, pp. 181-221.

Kuhn R. (2007), *Henryk Grossman and the Recovery of Marxism*, University of Illinois Press, Illinois.

Kuhn, R. (2016), 'Introduction to Henryk Grossman "The value-price transformation in Marx and the problem of crisis"', *Historical Materialism* issue 1, vol 24, Brill, pp. 91-103.

Lanchester, J. (2015), 'The Robots are coming', London Review of Books [online]. Available at https://www.lrb.co.uk/the-paper/v37/n05/john-lanchester/the-robots-are-coming (Accessed 14 November 2018).

Lawrence, M. (2014), 'Growing our way out of climate change by building with hemp and wood fibre', The Guardian [online].

Available at https://www.theguardian.com/sustainable-business/2014/sep/25/hemp-wood-fibre-construction-climate-change (accessed: 4 April 2019).

Lenin, V.I (1951 [1916]), *Imperialism: The Highest Stage of Capitalism*, Foreign Languages Publishing House, Moscow.

Lenin V.I. (1967 [1902]), *What Is To Be Done? Burning Questions of our Movement*, International Publishers, New York.

Lenin V.I. (1974 [1916]), 'Imperialism and the split in socialism', *Collected Works* vol. 23, Progress Publishers, Moscow, pp. 105-20.

Lenin V.I. (1974 [1915],) 'The Collapse of the Second International', *Collected Works*, vol. 21, Progress Publishers, Moscow, pp. 205-59.

Lenin, V.I. (1977 [1903]), 'The National Question in Our Programme,' *Collected Works*, vol. 6, 4th ed., Moscow, Progress Publishers, pp. 452-61; 'Does the Jewish Proletariat Need an 'Independent Political Party',' pp. 328-33.

Li, Y. (2020), 'This was the fastest 30% sell-off ever, exceeding the pace of declines during the Great Depression', CNBC [online]. Available at https://www.cnbc.com/2020/03/23/this-was-the-fastest-30percent-stock-market-decline-ever.html (accessed 24 March 2020).

Lui, J. (2019), 'Next China: The ticking debt bomb', *Bloomberg* [online].

Maito, E. (2014), *The Historical Transience of Capital: The Downward Trend in The Rate of Profit Since XIX Century*, Universidad de Buenos Aires, Munich Personal RePEc Archive.

Marx, K. and Engels, F. (1975 [1844]), *Economic and Philosophic Manuscripts of 1844*, *Collected Works* vol. 3, Lawrence & Wishart, London, pp. 229-326.

Marx, K. (1991 [1894]), *Capital* vol. III, Penguin Classics, London.

Marx, K. (1993 [1858]), *Grundrisse*, Penguin Classics, London.

Marx, K. (2009 [1875]) *Critique of the Gotha Programme*, Dodo Press, Moscow.

Marxist Internet Archive, 'The Programme of the Communist International. Comintern Sixth Congress 1928' [online]. Available at https://www.marxists.org/history/international/comintern/6th-congress/index.htm (Accessed 15 September 2020).

Mattick, P. (1971 [1969]), *Marx and Keynes: The Limits of the Mixed Economy*, The Merlin Press Ltd, Boston.

Mattick, P. (1981 [1974]), *Economic Crisis and Crisis Theory*, Routledge, London.

Mazzucato, M. (2018), *The Entrepreneurial State: Debunking Public vs. Private Sector Myths*, Penguin, Great Britain.

MIT Media Office (2012), 'How to turn leaves into solar panels,' EPFL [online]. Available at https://actu.epfl.ch/news/how-to-turn-leaves-into-solar-panels/ (Accessed 4 April 2019).

Mitlin, D., et al (2013),'Interconnected Carbon Nanosheets Derived from Hemp for Ultrafast Supercapacitors with High Energy', *American Chemical Society Publications*. Available at https://doi.org/10.1021/nn400731g

Morris, S.; Mooney, A. (2020), 'British banks warn BoE of pain of negative rates', *The Financial Times* [online]. Available at https://www.ft.com/content/f5339e6b-9bb4-48dd-8aad-aadd5f6f0d4f (Accessed 21 May 2020).

Murray-Smith, R. (2017), 'The hemp battery performs better than the lithium battery', Cannabis Tech [online]. Available at https://www.cannabistech.com/articles/the-hemp-battery-performs-better-than-the-lithium-battery/ (Accessed 2 April 2019).

Natural History Museum (2019), 'Leading scientists set out resource challenge of meeting net zero emissions in the UK by 2050' [online]. Available at https://www.nhm.ac.uk/press-office/press-releases/leading-scientists-set-out-resource-challenge-of-meeting-net-zer.html (Accessed 6 June 2019).

National Association of Manufacturers (2020), '2019 United States Manufacturing Facts' [online]. Available at https://

www.nam.org/state-manufacturing-data/2019-united-states-manufacturing-facts/ (Accessed 1 November 2019).

Neufeld, D., 'Visualizing the 200-Year History of US Interest Rates,' advisor.visualcapitalist.com, 1 October 2020.

Newman, P. (1987), 'April: Lenin re-arms Bolshevik vanguard: Russia 1917 part 3,' *Fight Racism, Fight Imperialism* 68. Available at https://www.revolutionarycommunist.org/socialism/4707-al040417 (Accessed 15 December 2020).

North Carolina Pedia, 'Population of the United States, 1790-1860' [online]. Available at https://www.ncpedia.org/media/population-united-states-1790 (Accessed 5 October 2020).

Norton, A. (2016), 'Automation will end the dream of rapid economic growth for poorer countries', The Guardian [online]. Available at https://www.theguardian.com/sustainable-business/2016/sep/20/robots-automation-end-rapid-economic-growth-poorer-countries-africa-asia (Accessed 20 March 2019).

Our World in Data, 'Government spending' [online]. Available at https://ourworldindata.org/government-spending (Accessed: 4 September 2019).

PA Media (2020), 'Bosses speed up automation as virus keeps workers home', The Guardian [online]. Available at https://www.theguardian.com/world/2020/mar/30/bosses-speed-up-automation-as-virus-keeps-workers-home (Accessed 20 March 2020).

Pento, M. (2013), *The Coming Bond Market Collapse*, Wiley, New Jersey.

Phillips, L. (2015), *Austerity Ecology & the Collapse-porn Addicts: A defence of growth, progress, industry and stuff*, Zero Books, Winchester (UK).

Phillips, M. (2020), 'Investors bet giant companies will dominate after crisis,' *The New York Times* [online]. Available at: https://www.nytimes.com/2020/04/28/business/coronavirus-stocks.html

Reid, A. (2020), 'Wall St. lays an egg: The Wall Street Crash, as viewed through the papers', Historic Newspapers [online]. Available at: https://www.historic-newspapers.co.uk/blog/wall-street-crash-newspaper-headlines/ (Accessed 18 January 2021).

Rehman, A. (2019), 'The "green new deal" supported by Ocasio-Cortez and Corbyn is just a new form of colonialism,' *The Independent* [online]. Available at https://www.independent.co.uk/voices/green-new-deal-alexandria-ocasio-cortez-corbyn-colonialism-climate-change-a8899876.html (Accessed 1 June 2019).

RethinkX (2020), 'We are on the cusp of the fastest, deepest, most consequential disruption of agriculture in history' [online]. Available at https://www.rethinkx.com/food-and-agriculture (Accessed 1 November 2020).

Richter, W. (2019), 'And the US Dollar's Status as Global Reserve Currency?', Wolf Street [online]. Available at https://wolfstreet.com/2019/07/01/us-dollar-status-as-global-reserve-currency-q1-2019/ (Accessed 2 December 2020).

Reuters (2020), 'Gold races to new record after blowing past $2,000 per ounce', CNBC [online]. Available at https://www.cnbc.com/2020/08/05/gold-markets-dollar-coronavirus-in-focus.html (Accessed 6 August 2020).

Reynolds, B. (2018), *The Coming Revolution: Capitalism in the 21st Century*, Zero Books, Hampshire (UK).

Rodrik, D. (2015), 'Premature deindustrialization in the developing world', Dan Rodrik's Weblog [blog]. Available at https://rodrik.typepad.com/dani_rodriks_weblog/2015/02/premature-deindustrialization-in-the-developing-world.html (Accessed 17 March 2020).

Schmelzing P. (2020), 'Eight centuries of global real interest rates, R-G, and the "suprasecular" decline, 1311–2018', Bank of England [online]. Available at https://www.bankofengland.co.uk/working-paper/2020/eight-centuries-of-global-real-interest-rates-r-g-and-the-suprasecular-decline-1311-2018 (Accessed 3 January 2020).

Shaikh, A. (1978), 'An Introduction to the History of Crisis Theories', *US Capitalism in Crisis*, New York, Union for Radical Political Economics, pp. 219-41.

Smith, J. (2012) 'The GDP Illusion,' Monthly Review [online]. Available at https://monthlyreview.org/2012/07/01/the-gdp-illusion/ (Accessed 1 January 2019).

Smith J. (2016), *Imperialism in the Twenty First Century*, Monthly Review Press, New York.

Smith, J. (2016), 'Why coronavirus could spark a capitalist supernova', Monthly Review [online]. Available at https://mronline.org/2020/04/04/why-coronavirus-could-spark-a-capitalist-supernova/ (Accessed 5 April 2020).

Smith, S. (2019), 'How to enjoy the end of the world', Youtube video. Available at: https://www.youtube.com/watch?v=5WPB2u8EzL8&feature=emb_title (Accessed: 2 December 2019).

Stalin, J.V., (1954), 'Concerning the International Situation', *Collected Works*, vol. 6, January-November 1924, Foreign Languages Publishing House, Moscow, pp. 293-314.

Stewart, H. (2015), 'Robot revolution: rise of "thinking" machines could exacerbate inequality', The Guardian [online]. https://www.theguardian.com/technology/2015/nov/05/robot-revolution-rise-machines-could-displace-third-of-uk-jobs

Strauss, D. (2020), 'BoE is financing UK's coronavirus measures, Bailey acknowledges', *The Financial Times* [online]. Available at https://www.ft.com/content/ad63e45c-ad55-41a2-ae2e-8d550ff0ac92 (Accessed 14 May 2020).

Summers, G. (2017), *The Everything Bubble: The Endgame for Central Bank Policy*, Phoenix Capital Research.

Surz, R. (2019), 'Per capita world debt has surged to over $200,000,' Nasdaq [online]. Available at https://www.nasdaq.com/articles/per-capita-world-debt-has-surged-to-over-%24200000-2019-07-24 Accessed 24 July 2019.

Szalay, E. (2020), 'Pound is becoming an emerging market currency, says BofA analyst,' *The Financial Times* [online]. Available at https://www.ft.com/content/4fd04fd9-7209-4b7c-97a1-97466f226159 (Accessed 24 June 2020).

Tarver, E. (2019), 'What Impact Does Inflation Have on the Dollar Value Today?', Investopedia [online]. Available at https://www.investopedia.com/ask/answers/042415/what-impact-does-inflation-have-time-value-money.asp (Accessed 14 December 2020).

Thorpe, S. (2015), 'Global debt is now 2.5 times the total money supply – the system is clearly unworkable,' Simon Thorpe Ideas [online]. Available at https://simonthorpesideas.blogspot.com/2015/02/global-debt-is-now-25-times-total-money.html (Accessed 1 October 2019).

Trotsky, L. (1933), 'The German Catastrophe: The responsibility of the leadership,' Marxist Internet Archive [online]. Available at https://www.marxists.org/archive/trotsky/germany/1933/330528.htm (Accessed 1 October 2020).

UK Hempcrete, 'Better-than-zero-carbon buildings' [online]. Available at https://www.ukhempcrete.com/services/better-than-zero-carbon-buildings/ (Accessed 2 April 2019).

USA Watchdog (2020), 'Michael Pento – This is a Global Depression,' Youtube video. Available at https://www.youtube.com/watch?v=v9cVxBX2bDE (Accessed 1 April 2020).

US Bureau of Labor Statistics, 'Consumer Price Index inflation calculator' [online]. Available at https://www.bls.gov/data/inflation_calculator.htm (Accessed 21 December 2020).

US Bureau of Labor Statistics, 'Percent of Employment in Manufacturing in the United States (DISCONTINUED),' Federal Reserve Bank of St. Louis [online]. Available at https://fred.stlouisfed.org/series/USAPEFANA (Accessed 10 September 2020).

US Bureau of Labor Statistics, 'Employment by industry, 1910 and 2015' [online]. Available at https://www.bls.gov/opub/ted/2016/employment-by-industry-1910-and-2015.htm (Accessed 12 January 2021).

Varoufakis, Y. (2015), *The Global Minotaur: America, Europe and the Future of the Global Economy*, Verso, London, third edition.

Washington's Blog (2011), 'The Average Life Expectancy for A Fiat Currency Is 27 Years...Every 30 To 40 Years the Reigning Monetary System Fails And Has To Be Retooled,' [online]. Available at http://georgewashington2.blogspot.com/2011/08/average-life-expectancy-for-fiat.html (Accessed 2 February 2018).

World Bank, 'World Bank data: GDP growth (annual %) - High income,' [online]. Available at https://data.worldbank.org/indicator/NY.GDP.MKTP.KD.ZG?locations=XD (Accessed 2 January 2021).

Yaffe, D. (1973), 'The Marxian Theory of Crisis, Capital and the State,' *Economy and Society* issue 2, pp. 186-232.

CULTURE, SOCIETY & POLITICS

Contemporary culture has eliminated the concept and public figure of the intellectual. A cretinous anti-intellectualism presides, cheer-led by hacks in the pay of multinational corporations who reassure their bored readers that there is no need to rouse themselves from their stupor. Zer0 Books knows that another kind of discourse - intellectual without being academic, popular without being populist - is not only possible: it is already flourishing. Zer0 is convinced that in the unthinking, blandly consensual culture in which we live, critical and engaged theoretical reflection is more important than ever before.

If you have enjoyed this book, why not tell other readers by posting a review on your preferred book site.

You may also wish to
subscribe to our Zer0 Books YouTube Channel.

Capitalist Realism
Is There No Alternative?
Mark Fisher
An analysis of the ways in which capitalism has presented
itself as the only realistic political-economic system.
Paperback: 978-1-84694-317-1 ebook: 978-1-78099-734-6

Rebel Rebel
Chris O'Leary
David Bowie: every single song. Everything you want to know,
everything you didn't know.
Paperback: 978-1-78099-244-0 ebook: 978-1-78099-713-1

Kill All Normies
Angela Nagle
Online culture wars from 4chan and Tumblr to Trump.
Paperback: 978-1-78535-543-1 ebook: 978-1-78535-544-8

Cartographies of the Absolute
Alberto Toscano, Jeff Kinkle
An aesthetics of the economy for the twenty-first century.
Paperback: 978-1-78099-275-4 ebook: 978-1-78279-973-3

Malign Velocities
Accelerationism and Capitalism
Benjamin Noys
Long listed for the Bread and Roses Prize 2015, *Malign
Velocities* argues against the need for speed, tracking
acceleration as the symptom of the ongoing crises of
capitalism.
Paperback: 978-1-78279-300-7 ebook: 978-1-78279-299-4

Meat Market
Female Flesh under Capitalism
Laurie Penny
A feminist dissection of women's bodies as the fleshy fulcrum
of capitalist cannibalism, whereby women are both consumers
and consumed.
Paperback: 978-1-84694-521-2 ebook: 978-1-84694-782-7

Babbling Corpse
Vaporwave and the Commodification of Ghosts
Grafton Tanner
Paperback: 978-1-78279-759-3 ebook: 978-1-78279-760-9

New Work New Culture
Work we want and a culture that strengthens us
Frithjof Bergmann
A serious alternative for mankind and the planet.
Paperback: 978-1-78904-064-7 ebook: 978-1-78904-065-4

Romeo and Juliet in Palestine
Teaching Under Occupation
Tom Sperlinger
Life in the West Bank, the nature of pedagogy and the role of a
university under occupation.
Paperback: 978-1-78279-637-4 ebook: 978-1-78279-636-7

Color, Facture, Art and Design
Iona Singh
This materialist definition of fine-art develops guidelines for
architecture, design, cultural-studies and ultimately social
change.
Paperback: 978-1-78099-629-5 ebook: 978-1-78099-630-1

Sweetening the Pill

or How We Got Hooked on Hormonal Birth Control Holly
Grigg-Spall
Has contraception liberated or oppressed women?
Sweetening the Pill breaks the silence on the dark side of
hormonal contraception.
Paperback: 978-1-78099-607-3 ebook: 978-1-78099-608-0

Why Are We The Good Guys?

Reclaiming Your Mind from the Delusions of Propaganda
David Cromwell
A provocative challenge to the standard ideology that Western
power is a benevolent force in the world.
Paperback: 978-1-78099-365-2 ebook: 978-1-78099-366-9

The Writing on the Wall

On the Decomposition of Capitalism and its Critics Anselm
Jappe, Alastair Hemmens
A new approach to the meaning of social emancipation.
Paperback: 978-1-78535-581-3 ebook: 978-1-78535-582-0

Enjoying It

Candy Crush and Capitalism
Alfie Bown
A study of enjoyment and of the enjoyment of studying. Bown
asks what enjoyment says about us and what we say about
enjoyment, and why.
Paperback: 978-1-78535-155-6 ebook: 978-1-78535-156-3

Ghosts of My Life

Writings on Depression, Hauntology and Lost Futures
Mark Fisher
Paperback: 978-1-78099-226-6 ebook: 978-1-78279-624-4

Neglected or Misunderstood
The Radical Feminism of Shulamith Firestone
Victoria Margree
An interrogation of issues surrounding gender, biology,
sexuality, work and technology, and the ways in which our
imaginations continue to be in thrall to ideologies of maternity
and the nuclear family.
Paperback: 978-1-78535-539-4 ebook: 978-1-78535-540-0

How to Dismantle the NHS in 10 Easy Steps (Second Edition)
Youssef El-Gingihy
The story of how your NHS was sold off and why you will
have to buy private health insurance soon. A new expanded
second edition with chapters on junior doctors' strikes and
government blueprints for US-style healthcare.
Paperback: 978-1-78904-178-1 ebook: 978-1-78904-179-8

Digesting Recipes
The Art of Culinary Notation
Susannah Worth
A recipe is an instruction, the imperative tone of the expert,
but this constraint can offer its own kind of potential. A recipe
need not be a domestic trap but might instead offer escape –
something to fantasise about or aspire to.
Paperback: 978-1-78279-860-6 ebook: 978-1-78279-859-0

Most titles are published in paperback and as an ebook.
Paperbacks are available in traditional bookshops. Both print
and ebook formats are available online.
Follow us at:
https://www.facebook.com/ZeroBooks
https://twitter.com/Zer0Books
https://www.instagram.com/zero.Books